how to
give
your
baby
encyclopedic knowledge

The Better Baby Press

Philadelphia, Pennsylvania

how to give your baby encyclopedic knowledge

More
Gentle
Revolution

Glenn Doman
Janet Doman
Susan Aisen

Design: Publication Services

Library of Congress Cataloging in Publication Data
Doman, Glenn J.

  How to give your baby encyclopedic knowledge

  1. Infants 2. Education, preschool 3. Child development
  4. Intelligence levels I. Title
                    83–73584
ISBN: 0–936676–34–5

The Gentle Revolution Series:

How to Teach Your Baby to Read
Glenn Doman

Teach Your Baby Math
Glenn Doman

How to Multiply *Your Baby's Intelligence*
Glenn Doman

The Universal Multiplication of Intelligence
Glenn Doman and J. Michael Armentrout

The Better Baby Encyclopedia *

Volume	I	*How to Measure Your Baby's Visual Intelligence*
Volume	II	*How to Multiply Your Baby's Visual Intelligence*
Volume	III	*Babies, Vision, and Intelligence*
Volume	IV	*How to Measure Your Baby's Auditory Intelligence*
Volume	V	*How to Multiply Your Baby's Auditory Intelligence*
Volume	VI	*Babies, Auditory and Intelligence*
Volume	VII	*How to Measure Your Baby's Tactile Intelligence*
Volume	VIII	*How to Multiply Your Baby's Tactile Intelligence*
Volume	IX	*Babies, Tactility, and Intelligence*
Volume	X	*How to Measure Your Baby's Mobility Intelligence*
Volume	XI	*How to Multiply Your Baby's Mobility Intelligence*
Volume	XII	*Babies, Mobility, and Intelligence*

*Currently being prepared.

Other Books by the Authors

What to Do About Your Brain-Injured Child
    Glenn Doman

Nose is Not Toes (A children's book)
    Glenn Doman

dedication

To the superb staff of The Institutes—
who are to a man and to a woman, physically
overworked, financially *underpaid,* and the
most *richly rewarded* people in the world—
working as they do—with the world's most
beguiling children.

acknowledgments

I wish to acknowledge the two groups of people who have made this book possible.

The first are my favorite people in all the world who I talk about at some length within the book itself. They are the people who have taught me everything which I know that is important.

The second group are the contributors who make up the deficits that the non-profit Institutes lose each year. I don't know what I would do without them since as the Chairman of the Board I am responsible for those deficits. They help me to preserve the pride which that percentage of my Irish corpuscles would otherwise find humbled by being forced to beg. I'm very grateful to them in all my corpuscles whether Irish or not.

Those splendid groups range from the United Steelworkers of America to the Sony Corporation, as well as splendid individual human beings who annually contribute amounts ranging from thirty thousand dollars to fifty cents. They have my eternal gratitude. What is more important to them is the perfectly splendid children their help makes possible, which is the only reward they have ever received, or wanted.

Glenn Doman

table of contents

a note to parents

Parents journey from every continent on earth (except Antarctica where I don't believe there are any children) to The Institutes for the Achievement of Human Potential in Philadelphia to attend a seven-day course entitled "How to Multiply Your Baby's Intelligence."

This course has been taken by many thousands of parents since 1975. This book is taken in its entirety from those lectures.

The authors are among the principal lecturers in that course which is presented by The Better Baby Institute of The Institutes.

While this book has been written by its three authors, not all the authors wrote all chapters. Most of the chapters were written by the Senior Lecturer, Glenn Doman, who is the Chairman of the Board of The Institutes. Other chapters were written by Janet Doman who is the Director of The Institutes and by Susan Aisen who is the Director of The Institute for Intellectual Excellence.

The reason for this is that in each case the author

is writing the chapter from his or her own lectures made so familiar by having given them hundreds of times to thousands of parents.

Just one more thing. In order to save the time required by saying mothers or fathers and tiny boys or tiny girls, we generally use mothers to mean mothers *or* fathers and we generally use little boys to mean boys *or* girls.

Seems fair.

Now you can get on to learning why it's a joyous and splendid thing to give your baby encyclopedic knowledge and precisely how to do it so that it *is* both splendid and joyous.

foreword

by Glenn Doman

Glenn Doman and students from the Early Development Program and The International School of The Evan Thomas Institute.

foreword

Welcome to the world of *The Renaissance Children* and to its inhabitants who are bringing about *The Gentle Revolution.*

If you are newly come to this extraordinary land of babies and tiny kids and are entering it for the first time through this book then let me be the first to welcome you and to introduce you to the inhabitants who are my favorite people in all the world. The odds are very high that you'll like them very much and that they'll like you as well.

There are a few people who don't like this new land but they are very few, mostly professionals who feel threatened by a world full of little kids who are highly capable, highly competent, and worst of all, very endearing.

But there are even some people who don't like rainbows.

It's a vastly exciting world. It's a thrilling, new, and wondrous world. As is the case in all worlds which are new, thrilling, exciting, and wondrous you will encounter delightful, charming, and beguiling people, facts, and events.

It's a good deal like going to Rio de Janeiro for the first time, or Mombasa, or to the Kalahari Desert, or to the Xingu or to Tokyo or to the Arctic. Only a great deal more so. For this new world is more than a single *place* or a *city* or even a *nation*.

It's a new *world,* like Space, except that this world, the world of the Renaissance Children, is much more a location in time than it is in geography. Like Space, it has always been there, available to whoever was bold enough, or wise enough, or accidental enough to enter it.

We entered it by accident, or at least almost by accident. We had already spent twenty years in another wonderful world in which we were searching for and finding ways to make brain-injured children able to walk and talk and to be intelligent when, almost by chance, we discovered this new world. I shall say in our defense that when we *did* discover it more than twenty years ago, we knew instantly where we were.

So—welcome to the world of the Renaissance Children.

If you are already a resident in this land, which is to say, if you have already taught your baby encyclopedic knowledge or to read or to do math or other wondrous things then you already know about the beguiling and soul-stirring place it is and in this book you will travel to places within which you may not have been before.

If you and your family already inhabit this good land then let me introduce the new mother to you and to the other neighbors.

As is the case in all new worlds, you learn most about a new land by getting to know the natives.

May I introduce to you the people in my world? There are four groups of them and they are my favorite people.

I would be hard put to rank those groups as to my *most* favorite group and in many cases they overlap so I'll list them in the order in which I first met each of the groups.

First, there are the astonishing brain-injured children and their indomitable parents. I have lived intimately with something more than twelve thousand such families starting with the first of them some forty-two years ago.

Second, there are the staff members of The Institutes, numbering about one hundred, most of them living but a few of whom have not lived to see the present glorious results, much of which are a result of their own brilliance. Chief among those who are gone but who will live forever in the generations of children whose futures they did so much to improve, were those genius physicians—Temple Fay, Raymundo Veras, and Evan Thomas.

The first members of the staff I met in 1941, with the sole exception of my wife, Katie, who I met in 1931 when she was eight years old and I was twelve.

Third, there are the beguiling Renaissance Children and their splendid parents. It is impossible to know how many of them there are altogether. There are about forty children and their parents who are a daily part of my life. These are the kids who are on the On-Campus Program of The Evan Thomas Institute. They range in age from newborns to ten-year-olds. These children are clearly truly Renaissance Children. They are kids for all seasons. They not only stagger my mind with their many-splendored excellence but they charm me endlessly and give me hope for this too often dreadful world.

There are also four or five thousand children whose parents have taken the seven-day "How To Multiply Your Baby's Intelligence" course given here at The Institutes for the Achievement of Human Potential in Philadelphia. The great majority of these children I have never met since the parents, who come from six continents, do not bring their children when they attend that course. They range in age from children who are not yet quite born (whose mothers were pregnant when they attended that course a few months ago) to children who are now twelve years old but who were five years old when their mothers or fathers attended that course seven years ago. Their parents were taught how to give their tiny kids encyclopedic knowledge, how to teach them to read, do math, learn foreign languages, play the violin, swim, do Olympic gymnastic routines, and a host of other lovely things. Those parents were told to teach their babies exactly as many of those things as they found joyous and were comfortable doing. Some of those parents found themselves being comfortable while teaching their kids to do one of those things for ten minutes a day. Others found themselves being not only comfortable but also enthralled with teaching their kids to do *all* of those things all day every day. As a consequence those children range from being above average to children who are also truly Renaissance Children. Some of these children I have met purposely or by chance. Five hundred of them are on The Institutes' Off-Campus Program and their families are in constant communication with us.

The last of these children range in number from a minimum of fifty thousand to a probable maximum of a half million. These are among the millions of children whose parents read *How to Teach Your Baby to Read* or *Teach Your Baby Math*. During the last twenty years I have actually had letters from more than fifty thousand mothers, thousands of whom reported the results in glowing terms. I have actually met only a few hundred of those children. Some of them are now in their mid-twenties and clearly they are now first-rate young adults with remarkable accomplishments, a keen-witted sense of humor, and are extremely pleasant people. I met the first of this group as tiny children twenty years ago.

Last, there have been and are the true geniuses I have been privileged to know. They are to a man and to a woman a joy to behold, to talk to, and to know. The majority of them I have come to know in the last fifteen years although I met and talked with Albert Einstein when I was seventeen years old but most certainly did not know him except, of course, through his work. Still I was, and remain, thrilled to have talked to him. He couldn't have been kinder to an eager but awed high-school boy. It was a proper introduction to genius.

Among the geniuses, who constitute the last group of my favorite people, are several Nobel Prize winners. Each of them, I've found, is able to explain to me what he's up to in fifteen minutes so that I can understand it, which tells us more about *them* than it does about *me*. It's the people below the genius level whose explanations baffle me. It's when you get down to the professorial level that I find myself almost totally befuddled. Most of my genius friends haven't got a Nobel Prize but *should* have. Some of them *will* have some day.

Perhaps altogether, I've got seventy true geniuses who are among my favorite people. Some of them are staff members or board members or parents. Several of them are kids. All of them are very different but all of them have a great deal in common. *All* of them have a keen sense of humor. *All* of them are extremely energetic, *all* of them are very sane, *all* of them are immensely secure. Perhaps most important of all is a fact that puzzles many people—*all* of them are simultaneously *passionate* about the things they believe and are very *gentle* people.

Most people believe that strongly held beliefs and gentleness are *opposite* characteristics. I have come to believe that in geniuses, they are *inseparable.*

All of the *myths* about geniuses propose just the opposite to these things.

All of the *facts* about geniuses show these things to be true.

All of the major advances mankind has made were first brought to light by geniuses.

The world does not suffer from too *many* geniuses, it suffers from too *few.*

My last group of favorite people, the geniuses I am privileged to know, are *all* in favor of more *knowledge* in the world, more *intelligence* in the world, more *ability* in the world and, most importantly, they are in favor of more knowledgeable and more capable children in the world.

In short, they have all contributed to and are in favor of The Gentle Revolution which is in the process of creating, through their parents, the delightful and capable children of tomorrow, the Renaissance Children.

Is it possible to create such children?

After forty years of eighteen-hour days and seven-day weeks on the part of the staff of The Institutes for the Achievement of Human Potential, we are absolutely persuaded of the truth of the most important single thing we have learned.

What we have learned is that:

Every child born has, at the instant of birth, a higher potential intelligence than Leonardo da Vinci ever used.

Intelligence is principally a product of three things:

the ability to read;
the ability to do math;
the amount of encyclopedic knowledge one has.

It is *easier* to teach a one-year-old to read than it is to teach a six-year-old.

It is *easier* to teach a one-year-old math than it is to teach a six-year-old.

It is *easier* to give a one-year-old encyclopedic knowledge than it is to give it to a six-year-old.

This book tells you exactly *how* to give encyclopedic knowledge to a tiny child starting at birth or at any time prior to six years of age as well as *why* you might like to consider doing so.

If it all sounds too good to be true, too dreamy, too Utopian, and maybe just a little scary (as all new places are to some degree) then let me introduce you to some lovely facts, a very hard-nosed *reality*, and some very real people with real names and real faces and real accomplishments.

If, at the end of this book, you find yourself excited, hopeful, but still thinking it's a little too good to be true, then why don't you come to The Institutes to see for yourself and to meet the people this book talks about. Thousands of parents before you have done so from all over the world. Or you just might try it on your tiny kid and see what happens. You have everything to gain—and nothing to lose, except a bit of time.

If, on the other hand, you can't wait to get started giving your baby encyclopedic knowledge about all the beautiful, exciting, lovely, fascinating things there are in the world, well—do it joyously—it's a marvelous thing to do.

In any case—welcome to the world of encyclopedic knowledge—and the Renaissance Children.

1
facts are
the knowledge base

by Glenn Doman

facts are
the knowledge base

Tiny children would rather learn than eat or play. You can teach them absolutely anything that you can present to them in an honest and factual way—and facts are the knowledge base.

FROM THE "HOW TO MULTIPLY
YOUR BABY'S INTELLIGENCE"
COURSE

Literally hundreds of thousands of parents have taught their babies to read since the publication of *How to Teach Your Baby to Read* more than twenty years ago. They began when their babies were a few months old, one year old, two, three, or four.

Literally tens of thousands of parents have written to us to report on the splendid results they have had from doing so. These letters constitute the greatest body of evidence in existence in the world to prove that babies *can* read, *love* to read, and do so with total understanding of what they have read.

If the reader has already taught his or her baby or tiny child to read, she (or he) will have not the slightest doubt that it will be easy to give that same tiny child encyclopedic knowledge at a speed which boggles the adult mind.

Babies can learn absolutely anything that you can present to them in an honest and factual way and they don't give a fig whether it is encyclopedic knowledge, reading words, math, or nonsense for that matter.

They'd prefer great things—reading, math, all the presidents of the United States, the nations of Europe, the great art of the world, the song birds of the eastern states, the snakes of the world, the kings and queens of England, the great music of the world, the international traffic signs, the dinosaurs, the state flowers, or *any* of the millions of fascinating things there are to know about on this old earth.

But they'll even take nonsense if that's all they can get.

Babies are learning every minute of every day and we're teaching them—whether we know it or not. The problem is that it may be bad to be teaching them if we don't know we are. We may be teaching them things we don't actually intend to teach them. Most often we are unintentionally teaching them things which aren't worth learning—or at least aren't *as* worth learning as the things they *could* be learning and learning much quicker and easier.

I wouldn't dare tell a mother or father what is good taste or bad taste—who am I to tell a parent that?

But after having lived nose-to-nose with more than twelve thousand families and having studied babies from the moment of birth in more than a hundred nations (ranging from the most primitive jungles, deserts, and Arctic wastelands to the most civilized capitols of the world) for more than forty years and having learned some marvelous truths about babies and tiny kids in the process—I feel a very strong obligation to tell all parents who'd like to know about it, that you can put quality in a baby's brain as easily as you can put in junk.

In fact, easier.

It is easier to teach a baby the great paintings of the world than it is to teach him cartoons. It is easier to teach him the great music of the world than it is to teach him jingles.

But I'm getting way ahead of myself and the reader as well.

You can teach a baby absolutely anything that you can present to him in an honest and factual way.

And facts are at the bottom of the whole business.

While the human brain is infinitely superior to all of the computers in the world tied together (as an example, all of the computers in the world could not carry on a free-flowing conversation in English at the level of an average three-year-old) and while the three-and-a-half-pound brain has a capacity thousands of times greater than *any* computer, there are nonetheless many similarities between the brain and the computer.

The computer, like the brain, is entirely dependent upon the number of facts it has stored in its memory.

In the computer each of those facts is called a *Bit of Information.* In a human child or adult we have chosen to call those facts *Bits of Intelligence.*

In the computer, as in the child's brain, the new knowledge which can be derived from those facts is limited by the number of facts which are stored.

In the computer the number of facts which are stored is called *The Data Base.* In the human brain we have chosen to call those facts *The Knowledge Base.*

And children learn those facts which we call Bits of Intelligence at a *rate* which no adult could come *even close* to equaling.

Do facts in themselves constitute intelligence?

No, of course they don't.

But they do constitute the base on which all intelligence is built.

With *no* facts there can be no intelligence.

With an average number of facts we have the base for average intelligence.

With a huge number of facts we have the base for high intelligence.

And for tiny kids, learning facts is as easy as duck soup and infinitely more fun.

The *younger* a tiny kid is, the *easier* it is to teach him facts.

Easier at five than at six, at four than at five, at three than at four, at two than at three, at one than at two, and easiest of all before one.

All you have to know is precisely *how* to do it and *why* you're doing it.

Let's talk about some very real kids who we get to see almost every day, about the facts they learned, how many facts they learned, how they put these facts together to come to *new* conclusions, how they used the interrelations *between* these facts to be extremely creative, and what these kids are like today.

First let's meet them. They are among my favorite people in the whole world.

They are the kids who are the student body of The Evan Thomas Institute.

They come in two groups. The first group is made up of the little kids of *The Early Development Program.* They range in age from newborns who were registered before they were born to five-year-olds. These children are taught entirely by their mothers who come to The Institutes once a week for a period of four hours to learn how to teach them. They then go home and, with Dad's help, they do the teaching and come back again the following week.

The present students in that program as of December 1, 1983 are:

Marlowe Doman	3½ weeks old
Shana McCarty	8 months old
Yuuki Nakayachi	9 months old
Nicholas Coventry	15 months old

David Burchfield	19	months old
Neal Gauger	20	months old
Zachary Lewinski	24	months old
Ginette Myers	26	months old
Christy Gerard	32	months old
Frederick Brown	35	months old
Christopher Coventry	3	years old
Christopher Barnes	3	years old
Christopher Cunningham	3	years old
Paul McCarty	3	years old
Michael diBattista	4	years old
Alison Myers	4	years old
Chloe Coventry	5	years old
John Brown	5	years old
Adriana Caputo	5	years old
Erin Burchfield	5	years old

Most of these children were registered before they were born (often because they had older brothers or sisters on the program) or during the first year of life. Some children enter later such as

Ryan Rossi	3	years old

who has just entered the program. Many of the children who enter beyond one year have already been taught at home by their mother. Some of the children are the children of staff members such as Marlowe Doman, Yuuki Nakayachi, Nicholas, Christopher, and Chloe Coventry. *All* of the tiny kids themselves are staff members in the very real sense that they, along with their parents, demonstrate for the parents who attend The Institutes' courses. The little ones below two demonstrate *how* they are taught by their parents and the kids from two years up demonstrate *what* they have learned.

What have they learned?

Well, what they have learned and learned joyously and eagerly, are facts—the facts that we call Bits of Intelligence. Taken together they add up to encyclopedic knowledge.

Facts, in order to be facts, must have these characteristics. They must be true (not opinions). They must be precise (crystal-clear, not approximations). They must be discrete (the fact alone). They must be unambiguous (named exactly) and they must be large enough to be clearly seen or loud enough to be clearly heard.

What are some facts?

A portrait of George Washington is a fact.

A painting such as the *Mona Lisa* is a fact.

The outline of the state of Pennsylvania is a fact.

The photograph of a copperhead snake is a fact.

A word is a fact, whether spoken or written.

The smell of gasoline is a fact.

A musical note whether sounded or written is a fact.

A numeral whether spoken or written is a fact.

Actual numbers whether spoken or printed are facts.

And so are hundreds of thousands of other things.

If they are presented singly and have met all the other requirements which we have described, then each fact so presented is a Bit of Intelligence.

The mothers of the Early Development Program begin the program as soon after the baby is born as possible, presenting those facts to their babies in the manner which will be covered in detail in later chapters. They do so with a good deal of pleasure and enthusiasm and the babies respond in the exact same manner and with the precise same degree of pleasure and enthusiasm as the parents put into the presentation.

What is the result of doing this?

Well, by two years (prior to their third birthday) virtually all of the children who started at one year of age or less have the following characteristics.

1. They know upward of four thousand Bits at sight. (Since they obviously know them both visually and auditorially that means *eight* thousand Bits of Intelligence.)
2. They can read at least four thousand words in two or more languages. (Since they obviously know these words both visually and auditorially, that means *eight* thousand Bits of Intelligence.)
3. They can read many books.
4. They have begun to play the violin.
5. They can do arithmetic.
6. They know the great paintings of the world and other art masterpieces.
7. They are familiar with the geography of the world.
8. They recognize the great music of the world. (They have been listening to tapes since birth.)
9. They can write.
10. They can speak and understand sentences in one or more foreign languages.
11. They can do a host of other things such as swim, dive, and do gymnastics (things which are not the subject of this book but which are covered in other books).

12. They are sweet, secure, and charming children who are immensely curious and who think that learning is the greatest game life has to offer.

They have in their possession scores of thousands of facts and have a voracious appetite to learn *all* of the facts there are in the world. They will never succeed in learning all there is to know in the world but they'd like to have a go at it. They believe that the world is a fascinating place to be and they think people are great.

2

I'd like you to know a few of my very favorite people

by Glenn Doman

I'd like you to know a few of my very favorite people

It is, in fact, nothing short of a miracle that the modern methods of instruction have not yet entirely strangled the holy curiosity of inquiry; for this delicate little plant, aside from stimulation, stands mainly in need of freedom; without this it goes to wrack and ruin without fail. It is a very grave mistake to think that the enjoyment of seeing and searching can be promoted by means of coercion and a sense of duty.

—ALBERT EINSTEIN

I'd like you to meet a very few of my very favorite people in all of the world. The truth is that I'd like you to meet *all* of my very favorite people. They fill you with hope for the world. But the constraints of a book prevent that, so let me pick a very few stories about a very few kids.

What are these children by the time they reach five?

By the time they are five years old they are superb children and are ready to enter The International School (if they and their parents wish them to do so).

By that time all of the children have these characteristics:

They read splendidly and have read hundreds or even thousands of books. One of the high points of my life occurred when a visiting television crew asked Heather McCarty (who is one of my favorite people in all the world), who was then four years old, what she could read.

After pondering the question for a moment to be sure she understood it, Heather said, "I can read anything."

After pondering her answer for a moment to be sure he understood it, the director picked up a book which was lying on a nearby table and asked her if she had ever read that book. Heather replied she had not.

The book was my own, *How to Teach Your Baby to Read.*

He thumbed through it and asked her to read the last paragraph in the book.

Heather read it.

Little children have begun to read and to increase their knowledge, and if this book leads to only one child reading sooner or better, then it will have been worth the effort. Who can say what another superior child will mean to the world? Who is to say what, in the end, will be the sum total of good for man as a result of this quiet ground swell which has already begun, this gentle revolution.

Heather read it quietly, clearly, and surely. She read it on camera. Then Heather smiled pleasantly.

The director cleared his throat and asked, "Heather, did you *understand* that?"

"Yes," said Heather, "except I'm not exactly sure what a 'ground swell' is."

I didn't actually see that last part since my eyes were covered by my handkerchief because I was blowing my nose—well, *sort* of blowing my nose.

I often have to blow my nose when beautiful little kids do things like that.

They have tens of thousands of Bits of Intelligence. (Shakespeare wrote all of his plays using a total vocabulary of less than 10,000 words.)

They have intuited (discovered) the relationships between those Bits of Intelligence in striking ways. As an example, most of the children have perfect pitch (which is actually the relationship between the Bits of Intelligence called single notes) and they are able to listen to classical compositions they have never heard before and to tell you who wrote them.

Another of my very favorite people in the whole world is Colleen Brown. Colleen knows many thousands of art masterpieces ranging from da Vinci to Picasso and Wyeth.

I remember a day, before Colleen was five years old, when, with her mother, she was demonstrating her Bits of Intelligence for the parents who were attending a Better Baby course. Mrs. Brown had brought fifty or sixty art masterpieces from the thousands of art Bits that the Browns have. Colleen was naming them happily and easily. After she had named the last of them, Mrs. Brown gave her five paintings she had never seen before and Colleen identified the painters.

To say that the parents who were attending the courses were impressed would be to state it mildly. What added to the depth of their impression was that these five paintings, each by a different artist, were in *black and white.* Everybody could see that I wasn't dreadfully impressed because I was blowing my nose again.

That's what happens when kids who have thousands of Bits of Intelligence start discovering (without anyone's help) the relationship between them.

Not only can they do mathematics (as can most adults) but they can actually *understand* mathematics (as most adults do *not*).

They play the violin, well.

They write books.

They write well.

They illustrate their own books.

They speak their own tongue fluently and articulately and at least one foreign tongue ranging from usably to fluently.

They read Japanese kanji *(which is the scholarly language of Japan) and many of them read more* kanji *than Japanese children who are three to six years older than they are.*

They do a host of other things splendidly, such as ballet and Olympic gymnastics.

Most important of all, they are the most endearing and captivating little kids I have ever met.

So stimulating and exciting are these little children and so capable are they that it is quite easy to forget that they are in fact five years old.

When Marc Mihai Dimancescu, who is one of my very favorite people in all the world, was five years old, he was playing the violin for a group of visitors.

He was playing it splendidly as he does everything. When he was through, a reporter asked him what the composition was that he just played.

"Gavotte," said Marc Mihai.

"Who wrote it?" asked the reporter.

"Lully," said Marc Mihai.

"How do you spell that?" asked the reporter, bending down so he could hear little Marc Mihai.

"L-U-L-L-Y," dictated five-year-old Marc Mihai.

I had tears in my eyes that time too, but they were tears of laughter.

The reporter said thanks and left but he didn't understand why I was convulsed. His own newspaper had carried a front page story a few weeks earlier which reported that more than thirty percent of all school children from ages seven to seventeen couldn't read and that every term students graduated from high school who couldn't read their own diplomas—or labels on jars.

I thought that contrast was funny—very sad at one end—but funny and wonderful at the other end.

Who *are* these kids who do such things? Did they

begin as genius children begotten by genius parents?

Nope.

If anyone thinks he can identify children as geniuses before they're born I have neither met him nor heard of him.

Are they average children now at five years of age? No, of course they're not. Do average five-year-olds do *any* of those things, never mind *all* of those things? They are certainly not average—but they are the way all kids *could* be. They are the way all kids *should* be.

Buckminster Fuller was a genius—and a friend of ours. Bucky was fond of saying that all kids are born geniuses and that we spend the first six years of their lives degeniusing them.

I would like to add that those first six years of life are *the* critical years because, by six, we have laid the groundwork for what we are to be.

Are these children not the genetic result of genius parents?

Well, they are *indeed* an unqualified product of their parents, but not a genetic product of their parents beyond the fact that their parents gave them the gift of life and the unexcelled gift of the genes of Homo sapiens.

But all parents give their children these two gifts.

Who *are* the parents of these kids?

Well, they have several things in common.

First of all they are firmly middle class in educational, economic, and social terms.

They range from blue-collar workers to professional people such as doctors, lawyers, and business people.

Their mothers range from high-school graduates, through college graduates, to the occasional mother with a master's or other postgraduate degree.

There are very few really rich people on The Institutes' programs. There are also very few really poor people. It's a sadness at both ends of the spectrum.

The rich, unhappily, have a false sense of *security* about their kids. Most of them believe that their wealth will provide their children with a guarantee of success and happiness. A few know better.

The very poor, unhappily, have a false sense of *insecurity* about their children. They have bought the

Rosalind Klein Doman and son, Marlowe, three and one half weeks old.

belief that their children really are innately inferior. A good many poor know better but don't actually know what to do about it.

So the largely middle class parents, who are giving their children the opportunity to be all that their virtually unlimited potential and their priceless gift of the genes of Homo sapiens gives them the right to be, have these characteristics in common:

They *love* their children very much (as do almost all parents).

They *respect* their children and their innate potential to be magnificent.

They *enjoy* their children immensely.

They have given their children a higher priority in their lives in terms of time and energy than have most families.

They do not feel this to be a sacrifice of themselves but rather a high privilege.

They think that it is more fun to teach their kids than it is to bowl or go to the movies.

They are more interested in their kids than they are in who shot J.R. or other "events" on television.

Does that mean they are not interested in world politics, the economy, the theatre, sports, art, music, literature, and the other good things in life?

Not at all.

They are a good deal *more* interested in those things than are average people.

They are lively, bright, aware, happy, effective people who are less involved in *worrying* about the world and a good deal more involved in *doing* something about it by raising happier, more effective kids.

But where do you find mothers who can read and write Japanese, teach art, history, geography, play the violin, give their kids encyclopedic knowledge on innumerable subjects, and do Olympic gymnastics, to name a few accomplishments?

Not a single mother of these kids could play the violin, had encyclopedic knowledge, could do gymnastics or speak a word of Japanese when they began the program except the mother Barbara Coventry, who teaches violin to the big kids (ages five to ten) in The International School; mother Patty Gerard, who teaches Olympic gymnastics to the big kids; and mother Miki Nakayachi, who teaches Japanese to the kids in The International School.

There's the *real* point from the parents' point of view. That's one of the main reasons *why* they're having the time of their lives teaching their kids.

In order to teach their kids some parents learned with the help of The Institutes' books which they got from the public library or bought. Some of them did only that.

Others of them made their own materials or bought The Institutes' already prepared materials.

Others actually attended The Institutes' courses and took it from there.

Others actually joined the On-Campus programs at The Institutes, by being in Philadelphia, or commuting from New York as did the Dimancescus or commuting from Mexico for months at a time as did the Carrencedos; some actually moved from England as did the Coventrys.

Obviously all of the families we are describing here did *all* of those things up to and including being enrolled in the On-Campus programs. Obvious also is the fact that all of these mothers have chosen to be full-time professional mothers.

The reader must also be made aware of the fact that there are hundreds, perhaps thousands of professional mothers who are raising superb children, who know all about The Institutes, and who have never set eyes on The Institutes or the staff. The vast majority of those mothers have used The Institutes' materials and books to do so.

Then there have been the mothers and fathers who have given their children the opportunity to be excellent who have never even heard of The Institutes or of The Institutes' books.

I learned about those parents during the early 1960s when the reading book first saw the light of day. They wrote to me to say that they had themselves taught their own babies to read and to do other lovely things using a method and material not unlike the ones we had designed. What was more, some of them had done so twenty or even thirty years earlier and they also reported to us the thrilling results in their now grown children.

They knew the *real* secret.

They knew that *the magic is in the child,* not in the materials.

They were proud of the materials they had designed as tools to teach their children just as we have spent a quarter of a century designing the tools which we use. They have the first-rate characteristic required which is the fact that those tools *work.*

But the *real* truth that they had learned individually was the precise same truth that we had stumbled onto and that truth is that *the magic is in the child.* Most specifically, the magic is in the child's incredible human brain.

That magic is especially potent in the years between birth and six, as we shall see shortly.

There have also been, long before The Institutes

or The Institutes' oldest staff member* was born or dreamed of, a thin line of individual parents who knew the truth. They knew it by instinct, or by their own genius, or by a series of brilliant insights, or by the sharpest of observations.

However they knew it, the fact is that they did, and knowing that, they did the things for their children necessary to produce most of the splendid people of history.

Back to the kids.

What happens to these captivating and endearing children when they get to be five?

A number of things.

A few of them have gone off to schools, ranging from public schools to very high-level private schools where most of them have gotten full scholarships and skipped a grade or two. Are they not then regarded as queer egg-heads by other children and their teachers alike?

Quite the contrary.

From the standpoint of the other kids, they be-

---

*Dr. Raymond A. Dart of *Australopithecus* fame and Dean Emeritus of the Medical School of the University of The Witswatersrand. Professor Dart is now 91 years old and is the Chairman of The Institutes' Institute of Man.

come the natural leaders of the group for the simple and obvious reasons that they are sweet, secure, and highly imaginative. It is not the bright, secure kids whom the class hates—it is the smart-alec, loud-mouthed, insecure kids who are disliked.

What kind of people do *you* pick for your friends?

From the teachers' standpoint they are ideal kids to have in class. They need little or no help, they help the other kids and give the teacher more time to spend with the kids who *can't* read or do arithmetic—who are the classroom problems, as every teacher with a grain of sense knows.

The rest of them, which is the majority of the kids who finish the Early Development Program, go on to enter The International School of The Evan Thomas Institute.

The present students of that school are among my very favorite people in the whole world and at the present time they include:

Michelle Gauger	6 years old
Vikki Barnes	6 years old
Heather McCarty	6 years old
Katie Brown	7 years old
Chip Myers	7 years old
Jason Sherman	7 years old
Colleen Brown	8 years old

Enrique Carrencedo	8 years old
George Koenig	8 years old
Cara Caputo	9 years old
Micah Sherman	9 years old
Marc Mihai Dimancescu	9 years old
Beatriz Carrencedo	10 years old
Mary Ellen Koenig	10 years old

Three recently admitted students who were entirely taught at home by their parents are:

Molly Ann Pereira	6 years old
Jock Pereira	8 years old
Joshua Pereira	10 years old

The children of The International School enter at five years of age.

This school is a regularly licensed grade school and all the children who enter can already:

1. Read two or more languages.
2. Understand and speak two or more languages.

(The native language is spoken fluently and the other language or languages are spoken ranging from usably to fluently.)

3. Do competent arithmetic.
4. Play a musical instrument or instruments well.
5. Have a huge store of encyclopedic knowledge.
6. Are physically excellent.
7. Do advanced gymnastics.
8. Have many additional splendid abilities.

The first graders attend school at The Institutes from nine to one o'clock.

The other grades attend from nine to three.

All grades continue to learn at home with their parents.

All of the children think that The International School is a great place to be.

There is a two-fold purpose in having told the parent who is reading this book about The Evan Thomas Institute and the Renaissance Children at such length and neither of them is to solicit applications for The Evan Thomas Institute.

The schools are very small by their nature and both have very long waiting lists.

The primary reason for the detailed discussion is to show the reader precisely what is possible with

perfectly ordinary little children of perfectly ordinary parents who have assigned their families and
raising their children a very high priority in life.

It is clear that families have various priorities in
life and that is a good and proper thing. It is one of
the things that makes life so rich and varied. I have
many dear, fascinating, and treasured friends who
have very different objectives for themselves and for
their children and I would not have it different than
it is.

This book and the work of The Institutes is directed towards those parents, and it is a very large
percentage of parents, who wish to devote a small
period of time a day, or an hour a day, or all day
long to have a personal and active role in teaching
their own children.

You can give your child precious knowledge with
the greatest of mutual pleasure in fifteen minutes a
day if you would like to do so and find honest happiness in the doing.

One of the things you can do with a small invest-
ment of time which is especially easy, especially
agreeable, especially valuable, and especially rewarding is to teach your tiny child about nature.

For him to know fifty common birds, fifty trees,
fifty flowers, fifty shrubs, fifty animals, fifty insects,

fifty animals, and fifty snakes will give him a lifetime of pleasure.

It will also bring him a good dose of respect from his peers at ages five, fifteen, fifty, and seventy because very few people know the creatures and plants which fill the state in which they live. It is more than strange that schools rarely teach nature study. Most First Class Scouts and all Eagle Scouts tend to know more about nature than do most college professors.

Another advantage is that in teaching your child the nature Bits of Intelligence you will even learn some of them yourself and get to enjoy the world around you a great deal more. You won't learn nearly as much or nearly as fast as your two-year-old, but in the process of teaching him you'll learn a great deal that you don't know now.

The second reason we have dwelt on the kids themselves at such length so early in this book is to give you some feel for the kids themselves.

We have talked not at all about the eight-year-olds and the other kids in The International School except to name them. I'm a little reluctant to talk about them in much detail because they are incredible.

Incredible means not believable. The trouble with telling people things that are unbelievable is that they don't believe them. It's a foolish thing to do—I try not to do foolish things.

I shall content myself (with a good deal of self-discipline) to tell you a couple of things about the kids in general and about a couple of the kids themselves which are believable, true, and illustrative of many things.

The children of The International School do all the things that the kids in the Early Development Program do, but they do them even better and they are even more engaging (although that seems impossible, even to me).

What most people find intriguing and surprising about them is that they have little if any competitiveness about them. They are extremely supportive of each other and applaud each other enthusiastically on every occasion.

There are many who believe that competitiveness is the *answer* to the world's problem. Others of us believe that competitiveness toward each other *is* the world's problem.

The boys and girls of The International School obviously believe in supporting *each other* and competing against *themselves.*

An example of this is when questions are being asked every hand in the room goes up eagerly. The hands shoot up not only before they have heard the *question* but often before they know the *subject*.

The College Bowls are a good example. One of the demonstrations that the kids of The International School put on for the parents who are attending The Better Baby Courses is the College Bowl.

The five- to ten-year-old students are considered staff members and they *earn* the right to teach in The Better Baby courses by performing optional tasks at home and in school.

For this particular demonstration they are divided into two teams for the purpose of answering questions on a variety of subjects. They have no prior notion of either the subjects or the questions which will be asked. Obviously they have studied the subjects, sometimes years earlier.

They decide on a team on the spot and choose two or three adults from the audience to be on each side and to "help" them with the answers. Team names chosen have included "The Base Sixes," "The Tigers," "The Exponentiationists," and "The Cookie Monsters."

The teams are asked questions alternately and there are many whispered consultations. Fortunately, coaching takes place on the teams which allows even some of the grownups chosen to "help," to give an occasional correct answer.

It is not uncommon for a child on "The Chipmunks" team to whisper an answer to a child on "The Logos" team. So much for competitiveness!

Typical questions are:

1. The rating P on the International Scale of River Difficulty means what?
2. *Cual es la Montana mas alta de Sud America?*
3. How many sharps in the key of D major?
4. To what kingdom, phylum, class, and order does the opossum belong?
5. What numeration system is broken the moment there are two ways to represent the same quantity?
6. *Samurai wa nani o motte imasuka?*
7. In what year was the comic opera *The Mikado* by Gilbert and Sullivan produced and who was the ruling monarch of Great Britain at that time?
8. What kind of micro-computer memory is lost the instant the computer is turned off?
9. In physics, what instrument is used to measure mass?
10. What artist was a close friend of Vincent Van Gogh's and quarreled with him shortly before Van Gogh cut off his ear?

That will give you an idea about the questions, each of which is a Bit of Intelligence.

If you are an average grownup or even an *above* average grownup, you may have gotten less than a perfect score. Few adults are well rounded enough to answer all those questions.

I got the one about Gilbert and Sullivan right in relationship to Queen Victoria but I was two years off as to the year. As for the other nine questions, I had trouble mostly because I didn't understand the questions.

I chose those particular questions in order to get around to telling you about a friend of mine named Micah Sherman. Micah is nine years old and, you'll be surprised to learn, is one of my very favorite people in the whole world. I chose those particular ten questions because I heard Micah answer every one of them correctly in one or another of the College Bowls.

My ambition in life is to grow up to be like Micah Sherman.

Micah can do everything.

He does everything splendidly.

Micah is a superb gymnast, *understands* mathematics, plays the violin well enough to entertain grownups at fancy dinners as a strolling minstrel, has an incalculable number of facts (Bits of Intelligence) at his disposal, speaks Spanish as fluently as he speaks English (which is very fluently indeed), writes computer programs, and runs marathons.

I can do *none* of those things.

You can see why I'd like to grow up to be like Micah Sherman.

Or his brother Jason, or Chip, or Enrique, or Marc Mihai, or George, or Jock, or Josh. They all do things like that and much more.

In the most recent College Bowl presented for the parents taking a Better Baby Course about three weeks ago, the kids had picked me to be on one of the teams. They had also picked one of the fathers attending the course who happened to be a mathematician. Micah was on our team.

One of the questions asked was, "What are the inside angles of a regular pentagon?"

I was a little vague about which *were* the inside angles (as opposed to the outside angles) but did some vague divisions in my head. I had a quick consultation with Micah and the mathematician father.

"I think it's about seventy degrees," I said.

"It has to be more than ninety degrees," said Micah and the mathematician simultaneously.

"108 degrees," shouted Micah, thus giving the correct answer to the other team.

"He's right," said the mathematician father with a broad smile on his face and surprise in his voice.

Another one of my favorite people in all the world is Cara Caputo. Cara is just nine years old.

One of the most interesting things about Cara is that Cara first joined the program when she was four-and-a-half years old.

That may be a vast relief to the parent reading this book who has begun to get the impression that his fifteen-month-old baby was over the hill. The earlier a baby starts the easier it is to learn, but Cara is glorious proof that the jig isn't up until six.

Cara can also do everything—and it is entrancing to hear her and to watch her.

In College Bowls I have watched her plot truth sets on the Cartesian plane for such equations as:

$$x = y + 14$$
$$y = 3 \times -2$$

I have watched her use the law for the multiplication of exponential terms to solve complicated problems.

I have watched her solve problems with substitutions using the distributive axiom for multiplication over addition.

Whatever *that* means.

Cara and her classmates were not *taught* the laws of advanced mathematics (remember what Einstein said), they *discovered* those laws by Socratic instruction, initially by the instruction of that genial genius, William Johntz, and later by Frank Caputo, who is a staff member and Cara's father.

Is Cara not therefore a squinty-eyed little egghead?

Cara, at nine years of age, is breathtakingly beautiful.

Recently the kids were doing a gymnastic demonstration for the parents of The Better Baby Course and, as usual, their performance was overwhelming.

Cara was stunning. Cara did an Olympic routine on the balance beam in which she had been instructed by her mother, Janet Caputo. Frank, Janet, Cara, and her little sister Adriana are together one of my very favorite families in the whole world. Cara had been polished in this routine by that beautiful world class gymnast Patty Gerard who, like the Caputos, first came to The Institutes as a parent taking the Better Baby Course.

As I watched Cara performing so skillfully, and so

gracefully, so completely in control of her body, half lovely child and half lovely young woman, my eyes filled with tears and I didn't even bother to blow my nose.

They were tears of appreciation—and of promise of tomorrow.

How easy it would be for Cara, eight years from now, to be at once an Olympic Gold Medal winner and Miss America in the same year. The only thing I was left wondering was, what would she do in the talent part of the Miss America contest? I don't believe the judges can give any contestant two weeks to demonstrate her "talents," much less the lifetime in which Cara will be using hers.

I don't believe Cara will want to do either of those things, for either of them requires an intensity of effort and a concentration in a single area that Cara's broad range of interests and abilities would probably exclude, for Cara is a Renaissance young lady, but isn't it nice that she could if she wished to do so?

The purpose of giving a child encyclopedic knowledge is not to make Nobel Prize winners, or concert violinists, or Olympic stars, or geniuses of any sort. It is to give them unlimited options in life. So few of us have had unlimited options. The purpose of giving a child every possible ability (and the possibilities are endless) is to give him unlimited horizons, to open all possible doors. It is so that *he* can *choose* what *he* is to be, from an endless list of possibilities.

I have another ambition after I grow up to be like Micah.

I want to run off with Cara Caputo, or Michelle, or Vikki, or Heather, or Katie Brown, or Colleen, or Beatriz, or Mary Ellen.

That one is going to be a little difficult since I already ran off with Katie Doman forty years ago.

All the kids are like Micah and Cara.

The basis of why they are the way they are, aside from the fact of their parents' love and respect for them, is the fact that they:

1. Are full to brimming with encyclopedic knowledge.
2. Read splendidly.
3. Understand math.

This book deals with how to give your baby encyclopedic knowledge. In order to do so you must understand two things.

The first is *why* you should do it.

The second is *how* you should do it.

The first thing is *why* you should do it and it is even more important than the second, so let's begin with why you should do it.

You should do it because it is the basis for all intelligence and intelligence is a birthright.

3

intelligence is a *birthright*

by Glenn Doman

intelligence is a *birthright*

Every child born has, at the instant of birth, an inherent right to be highly intelligent. It is not a right granted by the state, or the law, but is instead granted by the Highest Authority. It is a right endowed upon him by Nature itself; by the Creator, if you like.

Beside the right to be intelligent, all other rights fade into insignificance and can be exercised in only a limited way.

The degree of that limit is the degree by which intelligence is limited.

Intelligence is a birthright which transcends all other rights. Intelligence is a birthright conferred upon man as Nature's highest gift, his glorious gift of the genes of Homo sapiens—his only true genetic gift.

All other creatures of the earth, however beautiful or extraordinarily capable they may be, are in the end *specialists*. Man cannot (without his ingenious creations which are in themselves a tribute to his intelligence) fly like the eagle, swim like the shark, climb like the monkey, run like the cheetah, hover like the hummingbird, or even dig like the mole. These creatures, like all the others, survive by their own specialities. Their specialities have within them their own limitations.

If a creature less than man survives by climbing swiftly and easily into the trees to escape his enemies and does so splendidly, therein lies his own limitation. If due to changes in climate the trees disappear, so too does the creature who survives by climbing trees.

The dinosaurs were superbly adapted to their own environment and when that environment went, so did the dinosaurs; so also did thousands of other creatures as a product of their own specialities.

Man, on the other hand, is a *generalist,* as a product of his own intelligence. He is the only creature in the four-billion-year history of the earth who has within him the seeds of his own destruction—or his own exultation. Which of these extremes he will choose is also a product of his own intelligence.

For we holders of the precious gift of the genes of Homo sapiens are, taken at our worst, a dreadful lot indeed. For that intelligence, exercised in a limited and selfish way, has given us the ability to design weapons which gave "civilized" people the ability to kill more than fifty-four million fellow human beings between 1820 and 1945. What is more, we did so.

Taken at our most intelligent, selfless, cooperative best, we human beings are a superb, heroic, imaginative, adaptable, joyous bunch, touched at our best with a bit of divinity.

Which of those two wildly divergent creatures we will be tomorrow is a product—pure and simple— of our degree of intelligence.

Every child is born with the nature-endowed right to be intelligent.

Just a little over 207 years ago, a handful of superb human beings sat down, just eight miles as the crow flies from The Institutes for the Achievement of Human Potential, and changed the course of history.

They had dreamed a dream.

They wrote a document, a very short one, unrivaled in the English language not only for the superlative things it had to say, but for the simple elegance with which it said them.

> We hold these truths to be *self evident*,
> That *all* men are created equal,
> That they are *endowed* by their Creator
> with certain *unalienable* rights,
> That among these *are life, liberty,*
> and the *pursuit of happiness.*

The italics are, of course, my own. I would not dream of trying to improve upon that magnificent document, but only to emphasize the significance of what it says. Although I have known it by heart since I was eight, I am unable, even today, to say or write even a part of it without tears rushing unbidden to my eyes.

I have always treasured the belief that the giants who wrote it had taken for granted the *prior* right to be intelligent.

For without intelligence, there is no true life, liberty, or pursuit of happiness.

With limited intelligence, there is limited access

to life, to liberty, and to the pursuit of happiness.

With average intelligence, there is average access to life, to liberty, and to the pursuit of happiness.

With unlimited intelligence (which is every child's birthright), there is unlimited access to life, to liberty, and to the pursuit of happiness.

One hundred and sixty-five years later, and once again at a moment of earthshaking events, Franklin Roosevelt was inspired to propose to the Congress in his State of the Union message that:

> We look forward to a world founded upon four essential human freedoms.
>
> The first is Freedom of speech and expression—everywhere in the world.
>
> The second is Freedom of every person to worship God in his own way—everywhere in the world.
>
> The third is Freedom from want—everywhere in the world.
>
> The fourth is Freedom from fear—anywhere in the world.

I have also treasured the thought that President Roosevelt, like the Founding Fathers, also took for granted the *prior* right to be intelligent.

For without the right to be intelligent, freedom of speech, freedom of worship, freedom from want, and freedom from fear are mockeries, and hollow things indeed.

The most unalienable right of all rights for every newborn child is the right to be intelligent.

That right is inborn, it is implanted in the genes of Homo sapiens. It is his birthright.

All babies *know* it—innately.

All babies *demand* to be highly intelligent.

All babies *can* be highly intelligent.

All babies *could* be highly intelligent.

All babies *should* be highly intelligent.

That old genius, Buckminster Fuller, who is sorely missed by his friends of The Institutes, made to us, the last time we saw him alive, the statement we have already quoted. It is worth hearing again.

"All children are born geniuses and we spend the first six years of their lives *degeniusing* them."

Amen!

Bucky had been inspired to say it again, because he had just finished watching Marc Mihai Dimancescu who was, at the time, about five or six years old, teaching his classmates of The Evan Thomas Institute how to read C.A.T. scans of the brain.

Marc Mihai speaks and reads French superbly,

and with a flawless accent. Marc Mihai plays the violin in a way which invariably brings tears of pleasure to my eyes. Marc Mihai swims like a fish. Marc Mihai is an art expert. Marc Mihai does gymnastics well enough to impress the devil out of Olympic gymnasts. Marc Mihai does lots of other things astonishingly well.

Marc Mihai, in short, is just about like his classmates in The Evan Thomas Institute.

Marc Mihai is one of my favorite people in all of the world.

Babies would rather learn than eat.

Babies would much rather learn than play.

Babies think learning is a survival skill.

Learning *is* a survival skill.

Learning is how *knowledge* is acquired.

Knowledge *alone* is not intelligence.

Knowledge, however, is the basis of all intelligence.

Without knowledge there can be no intelligence.

This book tells you how to give your baby huge amounts of knowledge quickly, easily, and pleasurably.

The broader the base of knowledge a child has, the broader is his base for intelligence.

Did we remember to tell you that:

Every child born has, at the moment of birth, a greater potential *intelligence than Leonardo ever used.*

If we have mentioned it earlier, be assured that we will mention it again—and again.

It cannot be said too often.

What is intelligence anyway?

4

what do they do at The Institutes?

by Glenn Doman

what do they do at The Institutes?

Suppose that you had spent forty years of your life along with fifty to a hundred other people searching the world over to learn as much as you could learn about a subject and then found you could sum up everything you had learned in a single paragraph.

Would you find yourself vastly depressed that those thousands of people-years could be stated in a single, straightforward, rather short paragraph?

Or would you find yourself exultant that you had learned to state all that you knew in a paragraph?

That's what has happened to us.

Sometimes we see it one way and sometimes the other.

When we think of some of the hurt children whom we still fail to get totally well, I suppose that we most often think of all that we are still working on to find out about how the brain functions and tend to be upset that we can say it all in a single paragraph. (Although I have noticed that every time we make a new discovery and succeed with some of the hurt kids whom we had failed with up to that time, the new discovery still fits into the same paragraph.)

On the other hand, when we think of all the hurt kids who are now splendidly improved or totally well and when we think of all the magnificent kids who started out as average and who are now functioning beyond our wildest dreams of twenty years ago, we are inclined to think it's a pretty good paragraph.

The world has looked at brain growth and development as if they were predestined and unchangeable facts. We have discovered that brain growth and development are a single dynamic process. *This is a process which can be* stopped *(as it is by profound brain-injury). This is a process which can be* slowed *(as it is by moderate brain-injury) but most significantly, this is a process which can be* speeded.

Like it or not, this is what we have spent our lives finding out.

It may well be (with one exception) the most important precept we shall *ever* have.

If it *were* we are inclined to believe that it has been worth those thousands of people-years, for in that paragraph were the seeds of The Gentle Revolution.

But Hold! as Shakespeare was fond of saying, what good would such knowledge be if we then did not know what we could do with that knowledge?

And here we find that exception. Is there perhaps an even more important precept?

Happily or unhappily, depending upon whether we are looking backward or forward, we can also sum up all we have learned to *do about it* in a single paragraph.

It is difficult to say which of the two paragraphs is more important.

Which you see as the more important paragraph depends upon what kind of person you are.

If you are the sort of person who is made uncomfortable by doing things (however successfully) without understanding precisely why they work (as we are), then you will see the first precept as being the most important.

If, on the other hand, you are the sort of person who wants to get on with it and who is happiest when he sees splendid results being achieved (as we are) then you will see the second precept as being most important.

All we do at The Institutes is to give kids visual, auditory, *and* tactile *stimulation with increased* frequency, intensity, *and* duration *in recognition of the orderly way in which the brain grows.*

THAT IS ALL WE DO AT THE INSTITUTES.

Come to think of it, we don't even do that. What we *actually* do is to teach *parents* to do that.

That's *all* we do to make paralyzed children walk.

That's *all* we do to make speechless children talk.

That's *all* we do to make "mentally retarded" children intelligent.

That's *all* we do to make blind children see.

That's *all* we do to make deaf children hear.

That's *all* we do to make comatose children conscious.

That's *all* we do to make insensate children feel.

In a world which is positive that no severely brain-injured child can ever be made well it is not so surprising that we often *fail* to do so; what is surprising is that we often *succeed* in doing so.

George Bernard Shaw said, "One only has to see *one* white crow in order to know that not *all* crows are black."

We believe that one only has to see *one* severely brain-injured child who is now totally well to know that not *all* severely brain-injured children are hopeless.

That's also *all* we do to make average babies able to read several languages with total understanding by four years of age.

That's *all* we do to make average babies able to play the violin well by four years of age.

That's *all* we do to make average babies able to do splendid gymnastics by four years of age.

That's *all* we do to make average babies able to do advanced math by four years of age.

That's *all* we do to make average babies able to write computer programs by four years of age.

That's *all* we do to make average babies able to swim and dive by four years of age.

That's *all* we do to make average babies able to learn *anything* which you can present to them in an honest and factual way.

That's *all* we do to make average babies able to do *all* of those things by four years of age.

That's *all* we do to make average babies able to do all of those things *splendidly* by six years of age.

THAT'S *ALL* WE DO.

Or more accurately, we teach parents to do *all* those things.

That seems important enough to say one more time:

All we do at The Institutes is to give kids visual, auditory, *and* tactile *stimulation with increased* frequency, intensity, *and* duration *in recognition of the orderly way in which the brain grows.*

Can doing such a simple and straightforward thing actually accomplish such staggering end results?

Well, it does.

We see these things happening every day of our lives.

That question is asked us so often that we have learned to answer by asking a Socratic question, "How did Wilbur and Orville Wright know beyond a shadow of a doubt that it was possible for man to fly?"

Then the asker answers his own question, "Because they flew."

But *why* should doing such a straightforward thing have such staggering results?

My neurology professor taught me forty years ago and I have always supposed that his teacher taught him forty years earlier that, "If you want to increase central nervous system (the brain) transmission you do so by increasing the stimulus in *frequency, intensity,* and *duration.*"

Those three words, those three magic words, become three of the most important words in the life of the parent who wishes to give her baby the opportunity to learn how to do, and do splendidly, all the delightful, beautiful, and satisfying things there are to do in life.

Those three words:

Frequency
Intensity
Duration

take their place beside three other superb words which are guiding principles in dealing with a baby.

Those three other words are:

Love
Respect
Joy

But what of the rest of that paragraph?

Visual
Auditory
Tactile

There are just five pathways into the brain and everything Leonardo learned in his life, or you in yours, or I in mine, or your baby in his or hers, we have learned through those five pathways. Those five pathways are:

Seeing
Hearing
Feeling
Tasting
Smelling

Tasting and smelling are recessive pathways in man. Our pets, the dogs and cats, do them better then we do, and adults use them primarily as pleasure-seeking pathways. As a result we have dealt with them in other books.

These five pathways taken together form the sensory pathways which actually make up virtually the entire back half of the brain and spinal cord.

Never forget that when you are giving a child visual, auditory, and tactile stimulation with increased frequency, intensity, and duration that you are actually *physically growing* his brain.

We have never met a neurophysiologist who *didn't* know that—as we have rarely met a professional person who actually deals with kids who *did.*

If you feel that you understand what has been said in this chapter you are about ready to actually begin to learn how to give your baby encyclopedic knowledge.

It is also *all* that we do to give a baby encyclopedic knowledge.

5

intelligence has three legs

by Glenn Doman

intelligence has three legs

What actually *is* intelligence?

The Institutes people have spent more than forty years studying that question among tens of thousands of children and adults in more than a hundred nations, ranging as they have from the most civilized of places and people to the most primitive of places and people.

We have studied literally hundreds of definitions

given by dictionaries, encyclopedias, groups, and individuals.

They range, in our opinion, from *nonsense* to *interesting*.

We have found none of them to be *satisfying*.

While we have been engaged in actually *raising* the intelligence of children for most of those forty years, sometimes by more than a hundred points (in children diagnosed as having zero intelligence), we have never, up to now, defined it.

We have described it, illustrated it, discussed it at great length, dissected it, measured it exactly, and most importantly we have *raised* it, but we have never actually defined it.

In this chapter, for the first time, we shall offer a definition of it.

Had we actually raised their intelligences from zero to 100 (average) or more?

We could make a strong case that we had, in fact, done so. If the world regarded such a child as having an I.Q. of zero and dealt with him as having an I.Q. of zero and, as a consequence, had done nothing about him, would he not have continued to look, act, and be regarded as an idiot? If the world *now* agreed that his intelligence was average or above could we not claim to have raised his intelligence by 100 points or more? This has not happened once, but *many* times.

We could also make a strong case that we had *not* raised his intelligence by 100 points or more. Perhaps we had not raised it at all. Perhaps he had been misdiagnosed. Perhaps, having initially been speechless and unable to function, he had had no way to demonstrate his intelligence or to use it (other than internally) and had thus been regarded as an idiot. It is fair to ask: if Leonardo had been paralyzed and speechless and thus unable to *demonstrate* his intelligence, would he not have been regarded as an idiot? Perhaps even *fairly* regarded as an idiot, having accomplished nothing in his life.

This raises two essential questions about intelligence, or more accurately about intelligence *testing*, which is a *very* different subject.

Should we not divide intelligence into two kinds, first: *Functional Intelligence* (the way a child functions or fails to function prior to that situation being changed) and second: *Potential Intelligence* (the way he is capable of functioning if given full opportunity to do so). Our work with hurt kids over the last forty years and with well babies and tiny kids over the last quarter of a century proves beyond any reasonable question that there is in *all* children a tremendous gap between their Functional Intelligence and their Potential Intelligence.

The second question raised is that of the validity of intelligence tests or even whether they are useful. They are, in fact, often *harmful.* While it is true that people of demonstrated high ability very frequently score highly on intelligence tests it is *not* true that *all* people of high ability score highly on intelligence tests, any more than it is true that all people who score highly on intelligence tests demonstrate high ability in life.

Show us the high-level genius (as demonstrated by extremely high scores on intelligence tests) who in life is a bumbling ineffectual human being and we will show you that person as a perfect example of what is wrong with intelligence testing.

Show us the highly effective human being who accomplishes great things for the world but who does not score especially high on intelligence tests and we will show you that person as a perfect example of what is wrong with intelligence testing.

Intelligence has little, and sometimes nothing, to do with tests and has everything to do with accomplishments.

How then do we recognize our geniuses and who is your own favorite genius? Is it Leonardo? Shakespeare? Newton? Beethoven? Edison? Rembrandt?

Jefferson? Churchill? Bach? Gainesborough? Einstein? Michelangelo? W. S. Gilbert? Arthur Sullivan? Socrates?

Not one of them ever took an intelligence test.

Intelligence tests were invented during World War I as a means of *predicting* accomplishment. Sometimes they do. Sometimes they don't.

How then have we recognized our geniuses?

We have recognized them on the basis of *one* thing alone, we have known them on the basis of *one* thing alone. We have recognized them on the basis of *accomplishment,* the only thing which truly matters or ever has.

If we had been able to give Leonardo an I.Q. test and if he had scored 98, would the *Mona Lisa* not have been beautiful? If Thomas Edison had scored only 110, would the electric light bulbs have only lit up a little bit? If Newton had scored 87 on his I.Q. test, would apples thereafter have fallen upward?

Intelligence is nothing more and nothing less than how a human being's abilities compare with those of average ability (average being called 100).

This is quite difficult to see and measure in adults and quite easy to see and measure in children under six years of age.

There are precisely six things that characterize

human beings. Those six functions are all functions of the human cortex. Only human beings, among all creatures, have a human cortex in their brains, only human beings can perform the six functions that are the responsibility of the human cortex. Those six functions are:

1. The ability to walk, run, and jump in an upright position using arms and legs in a cross-pattern movement.
2. The ability to talk in an abstract, symbolic, conventional language which we have invented (English, French, Spanish, Swahili, etc.).
3. The ability to oppose thumb to forefinger in such a way as to write that abstract, symbolic, conventional language which we have invented.

These first three functions of the exclusively human cortex are all motor in nature and entirely dependent upon the second three, which are all sensory in nature.

4. The ability to see in such a way as to read that abstract, symbolic, conventional language which we have invented.
5. The ability to hear in such a way as to under-

stand that abstract, symbolic, conventional language which we have invented.

6. The ability to feel an object, without seeing it, tasting it, or hearing it and to know positively what it is.

These then are six exclusively human competencies which are confined to human beings. They are all functions of the exclusively human brain cortex.

These are:

Human Mobility Competence
Human Language Competence
Human Manual Competence
Human Visual Competence
Human Auditory Competence
Human Tactile Competence

These are all completely functional in an average child in our society by six years of age.

Thus a six-year-old child in a modern nation is expected to be able to walk, talk, write, read, understand his language through his ear, and be able to name a familiar object by feeling it, by six years of age.

He will, of course, go on to multiply those functions as he grows to be an adult but these will be lateral multiplications rather than new accomplishments, as he increases his reading, his understanding, and his motor skills.

A child who performs these functions precisely with his six-year-old peers will be in school with his peers (and will have an I.Q. of precisely 100).

A child who fails to do these things with his peers will *not* be in school with his peers. (If he does not accomplish these things until he is precisely twelve years old he will have an I.Q. of 50.)

A child who does these six things a good deal earlier than his peers will be in an advanced class. (If he accomplishes all of those things at precisely three years of age he will have an I.Q. of 200.)

Because there are six of these functions in human beings, it follows that there are six kinds of human intelligence.

These are:

1. Mobility Intelligence (Leonardo and Nadia Comaneci)
2. Language Intelligence (Leonardo and Winston Churchill)
3. Manual Intelligence (Leonardo and Andrew Wyeth)

4. Visual Intelligence (Leonardo and Pablo Picasso)
5. Auditory Intelligence (Leonardo and Eugene Ormandy)
6. Tactile Intelligence (Leonardo and Auguste Rodin)

This book does not concern itself with all of these kinds of intelligence but rather with what most people mean when they talk about intelligence, which is to say *intellectual* intelligence. Other books by The Institutes' staff deal with each of the kinds of intelligence.

We shall confine ourselves in this book to that intellectual intelligence.

Intelligence is a three-legged stool. It is achieved through:

Reading ability
Gaining encyclopedic knowledge
Doing mathematics

It therefore involves primarily

Visual intelligence
Auditory intelligence
Language intelligence

All of these abilities can be brought to the average six-year-old level in any average baby by three years of age. For parents who wish to do so this can be, indeed *must* be, a joyous and exciting experience for both parent and child. It can also take less actual time than is required to keep the child happy doing less joyous, interesting, and useful things.

The purpose of this book is to teach parents how to give their babies thousands or even tens of thousands of clear, precise, discrete, and unambiguous facts which are true, often beautiful, and always fascinating.

A child who by three years of age has a huge knowledge bank will be seen to be highly intelligent.

The child who continues to fill that knowledge bank, by six years of age (by which time the ability to take in information without the slightest effort will be essentially over) will be seen as being highly intelligent and will have the base required for extremely high intelligence and ability as an adult.

If he also reads at very advanced levels and does math with great ease, his parents will have given him an endowment beyond all the earth's riches or the highest social position. Unlike riches or social position it can not be taken from him.

What will high intelligence mean to him?

Now we shall define intelligence for the first time after forty years of search.

Intelligence is the degree of ability one has—to see the difference between the way things are *and the way things* could be *and to* make *them closer to the way they could be.*

That's what Leonardo did.

That's what Shakespeare did.

That's what Jefferson did.

That's what Rembrandt did.

That's what Edison did.

That's what Gilbert and Sullivan did.

That's what all the geniuses did.

That's what the Renaissance children of The Evan Thomas Institute are in the process of doing.

We find *that* satisfying!

6

how to teach your baby bits of intelligence

by Janet Doman
Susan Aisen

how to teach your baby bits of intelligence

The world is so full of a number of things I am sure we should all be as happy as kings.

—ROBERT LOUIS STEVENSON

The acquisition of knowledge is, in an intellectual sense, the objective of life. It is knowledge from which all else springs—science, art, music, language, literature, and all else that matters to man.

Knowledge is based on information and information can be gained only through facts. Those *facts* are single bits of information. When those facts are presented to a child in a proper way they become

Bits of Intelligence both in the sense that each of them literally grows his brain and in the sense that they are the base of all his future knowledge. This chapter will take the parent and the child through Bits of Intelligence, and thus lead the way to all *knowledge*.

This chapter is written as if it were addressed to full-time professional mothers* so that there are no limits as to what the parent who actually *is* a professional mother can do. It should in no way intimidate the mother who has very small amounts of time to spend with her baby. For her it simply means that her program will be spread over a longer period of time. Isn't it wonderful that there is more to learn than we can learn in a lifetime? How sad it would be were it the other way around.

The program of encyclopedic knowledge should be begun as soon as possible and may be carried on concurrently with the reading program. Those two programs are clearly the most important of all. These programs are the most fun and will provide the child with the most pleasure throughout life, encompassing, as they do, art, music, nature, biology, history, and all the other bewitching things life has to offer. Mothers should be well launched into

*By full-time professional mothers we mean mothers who are lucky enough to be with their babies full time and who wish to do so.

their Bits and into reading before intermixing math.

This chapter will cover:

What are Bits of Intelligence?
What are Categories of Intelligence?
How to teach Bits of Intelligence

WHAT IS A "BIT OF INTELLIGENCE"?

A Bit of Intelligence is one bit of information. A Bit of Intelligence is made using a very accurate drawing or illustration or excellent quality photograph. It has certain very important characteristics. It must be precise, discrete, unambiguous, and new. It must also be large and clear.

Precise

When we say *precise* we mean accurate and appropriate detail. It should be as exact as we can humanly make it.

If the Bit of Intelligence is a portrait of George Washington, it must be a very good one.

Discrete

When we say *discrete* we mean one item. There should only be one subject on a Bit of Intelligence.

If the Bit of Intelligence is the portrait of Washington, it must not also have in it other people.

Unambiguous

When we say *unambiguous* we mean named specifically with a certainty of meaning. Therefore each Bit of Intelligence is given a label that can be interpreted in only one way.

If it is a portrait of Washington, it must be labeled "George Washington" precisely and not labeled as "a president."

New

When we say *new* we mean something your child does not already know.

The painting on the next page is entitled, "Scene at The Signing of the Constitution of the United States" and George Washington is one of the most

The Scene At The Signing of the Constitution of the United States

prominent figures in the painting. If this painting by Howard Chandler Christy were used as a Bit of Intelligence entitled "George Washington" it would be a very incorrect Bit of Intelligence, since it would not meet the requirements for a Bit.

1. It would not be precise. That is to say it is *not* a painting of George Washington, it is a painting of the signing of the Constitution.
2. It would not be discrete. That is to say it is *not* a painting of one item (George Washington), it is a painting of many people.
3. It would not be unambiguous. It would be highly ambiguous since the child would have the right to believe that "George Washington" was a group of men scattered about a room.

The painting on the preceding page would be a perfectly fine Bit if it were part of a Category entitled "Famous Historic Events."

The portrait on the next page illustrates a correct Bit of Intelligence. The painting is *precise* because the portrait shown is detailed and clearly painted and is of George Washington.

It is *discrete* because there is only one subject represented.

It is *unambiguous* because there can be no question that it is George Washington and would be correctly labeled as such on the reverse side of the Bit.

Therefore—any proposed piece of information, to be truly a Bit of Intelligence for your child, must pass these six tests:

1. It must have accurate detail.
2. It must be one item only. It must not have a confusing background.
3. It must be specifically named.
4. It must be new.
5. It must be large.
6. It must be clear.

If any one of those characteristics is missing, it is not a suitable Bit of Intelligence and should not be included in this program. If all those characteristics are present, then it is a suitable Bit of Intelligence and will be easily learned by your child when done as part of this program.

Please make sure that you understand completely what a Bit of Intelligence is before beginning to put together and organize your program.

George Washington

CATEGORIES OF BITS OF INTELLIGENCE

It is clear from the definition of a Bit of Intelligence that any piece of new information that can be presented precisely, discretely, and unambiguously is the basic building block of intelligence. The mortar that holds that structure together is the categorization of Bits of Intelligence.

A Category is a group of ten or more Bits of Intelligence which are directly related to each other. For example "Insects" is a Category.

INSECTS

1. Two-Spotted Ladybird Beetle
2. Giant Walking Stick
3. Dragonfly
4. Housefly
5. Grasshopper
6. Ant
7. Termite
8. Periodical Cicada
9. Monarch Butterfly
10. Bumblebee

This Category of insects may be expanded to include every insect that ever lived from prehistoric insects up to the present or it may stop after thirty insects. In short, a category contains no less than ten Bits of Intelligence and is limited in breadth only by the number of species or members that exist in that group.

For example, as of 1983 the number of people who had been president of the United States is forty. The Category of presidents of the United States will only expand as new presidents are elected.

WHY RELATED BITS OF INTELLIGENCE?

This seemingly simple organizational detail has a profoundly important effect on the tiny child. If we present a tiny child with ten unrelated Bits of Intelligence which are each precise, discrete, unambiguous, and new we have given him ten superb pieces of knowledge. That is a marvelous thing to do. He will have these ten facts forever.

If you do it correctly you can show those ten cards to a tiny baby in ten seconds. Taking thirty seconds is far too slow to keep his attention.

That's a perfectly marvelous thing to do and, when you use ten seconds in such a way three or four times, he will have the information cold and for the rest of his life, if you review it now and then.

But in the precise same ten seconds we can give him ten related true Bits of Intelligence which will give him a minimum of more than 3,600,000 connections* to be his for all his life, which is a joyous and incredible thing to do, and that, Dear Reader, is why we use Bits in Categories.

We call these related Bits: Categories of Intelligence.

CHOOSING CATEGORIES

We have chosen to divide all existing knowledge into ten divisions:

1. Biology
2. History
3. Geography
4. Music
5. Art
6. Mathematics
7. Human Physiology
8. General Science

*See Chapter IX, "Millions of Connections in Thirty Seconds" for the explanation of more than 3,600,000. Don't read ahead now, just wait until you get to that chapter.

9. Language
10. Literature

Obviously we could have placed all information in five divisions, or a hundred. Why we have chosen these divisions will become clear as we proceed.

It should be your objective to give your child the broadest foundation of knowledge that you can provide. You would be wise to choose one Category from each of the ten divisions of knowledge above when you begin. Here are some examples:

Division:	Biology
Category:	Insects
Bits of Intelligence: (These are pictures of the insects themselves.)	Two-Spotted Ladybird Beetle Giant Walking Stick Dragonfly Housefly Grasshopper Ant Termite Periodical Cicada Monarch Butterfly Bumblebee (et cetera)

Division:	History
Category:	Great Inventors
Bits of Intelligence: (These are pictures of the inventors.)	Thomas Edison
	Alexander Graham Bell
	Guglielmo Marconi
	James Watt
	Benjamin Franklin
	Johannes Gutenberg
	George Washington Carver
	Wright Brothers
	Samuel Morse
	Eli Whitney
	(et cetera)

Division:	Geography
Category:	Countries of the Americas
Bits of Intelligence: (These are outlines of the shapes of the states.)	Canada The United States of America Mexico Guatemala Honduras Belize El Salvador Costa Rica Nicaragua Panama (et cetera)

Division:	Music
Category:	Musical Instruments
Bits of Intelligence: (These are pictures of the musical instruments themselves.)	Piano
	Violin
	Guitar
	Flute
	Oboe
	French Horn
	Trombone
	Clarinet
	Drum
	Cello
	(et cetera)

Division:	Art
Category:	Great Art Masterpieces
Bits of Intelligence: (These are reproductions of these paintings.)	*Sunflowers in a Vase* *Three Musicians* *The Mona Lisa* *View of Mount St. Vittoire* *Aristotle Contemplating Bust of Homer* *Holy Family* *Study of a Hare* *Portrait of Erasmus* *Maria de Medici* *The Wedding* (et cetera)

Division:	Human Physiology
Category:	Organs of the Body
Bits of Intelligence: (These are drawings of these organs.)	Brain
	Lungs
	Stomach
	Liver
	Kidneys
	Pancreas
	Heart
	Bladder
	Ovaries
	Testicles
	(et cetera)

Division:	Mathematics
Category:	Geometric Shapes
Bits of Intelligence: (These are drawings of the shapes.)	Cube Tetrahedron Octahedron Dodecahedron Icosahedron Sphere Cylinder Cone Pyramid Prism (et cetera)

Division:	General Science
Category:	Great Inventions
Bits of Intelligence:	Gutenberg's printing press
(These are drawings or photos of the inventions.)	telescope
	steam engine
	cotton gin
	spinning jenny
	telegraph
	typewriter
	mechanical reaper
	elevator
	telephone
	(et cetera)

Division:	Language
Category:	Food
Bits of Intelligence: (These are photos with words in ten different languages on the opposite side of the cards.)	apple strawberry banana egg milk bread carrot cabbage onion rice (et cetera)

Barbara DiBattista and son, Michael, 30 months old.

Photograph by Sherman Hin

Division:	Literature
Category:	Writers of Children's Literature
Bits of Intelligence: (These are portraits or photos.)	William Blake
	Ogden Nash
	Henry Wadsworth Longfellow
	William M. Thackeray
	Edward Lear
	John Keats
	Percy Bysshe Shelley
	Sir Walter Scott
	Walter de la Mare
	Aesop
	(et cetera)

Your child's intellectual diet should be a broad one. The more Categories that are taught, the wider view your child has of the world. It is not our intention to steer our children in one direction or the other—quite the reverse. We wish to offer them a sampler of the whole world. It will then be up to them to decide what directions they wish to take. But these decisions will be made on the basis of broad knowledge rather than on the basis of broad ignorance. Unlike most of us they will choose many areas from a spectrum of areas of competence, instead of eliminating vast areas due to incompetence.

HOW TO TEACH BITS OF INTELLIGENCE

The following section has been written to assist you in teaching Bits of Intelligence to your child. Although this technical information is important for you to know, the most vital and valuable ingredient in your program is within you. It is the affection and respect with which you teach. This technical information is to help insure that the intimate relationship you and your child share will be continually developing and growing through the teaching process.

Don't worry yet as to the exact nature of the Bit

Andrea Hines and son, Andrew, six months old.

Photograph

itself. You will learn all about that later. Suffice it to say that each Bit is on a piece of stiff poster board with the picture on one side and its name on the other side facing you.

You choose the first Category that you would like to show to your child. That Category contains ten Bits of Intelligence.

ONE SESSION

You position yourself and your child comfortably facing each other. You need to be able to show the cards about 18″ away from your child.

You begin by announcing joyously, "I have some insects to show you!" Then as quickly as your fingers will allow you, move the back Bit in the stack to the front and say, "This insect is a two-spotted ladybird beetle"; "This insect is a giant walking stick"; "This insect is a dragonfly." By taking the back Bit and moving it to the front you get a quick look at the name you are about to say. Then as you put that Bit out front you give your child its name. With high enthusiasm you zoom through these ten cards. Your goal is to do them as fast as you possibly can. This should take 10--15 seconds—certainly no more than that. One second for each card—and five seconds for you to fumble the cards. You'll quickly become as skilled as a blackjack dealer in Las Vegas.

For the first few days after introducing a new Category you should continue to say, "This insect is a [*name*]," but after that time say only "two-spotted ladybird beetle," "giant walking stick," "dragonfly," et cetera, as fast as you can. Kids catch on to the rules *very* quickly.

It is very wise to make sure all your Bits are right-side-up and turned label side toward you *before* you begin so that none of your child's time is wasted while you straighten out cards. Also, you should reshuffle the cards after each session so they are not being shown in the same order each time.

As you are aware from teaching your child to read you need to eliminate distractions from the environment. This is especially true when you are doing anything new for the first time. So when you begin your Bits of Intelligence Program be especially careful to create a quiet and nonchaotic time to introduce your Bits.

Frequency

It is important to space your Bits sessions during the day so you are truly doing many brief sessions rather than sessions back to back, which creates long sessions. Intersperse them with reading sessions; after you have completed a session go to something else. If your child cries "more" (as very often he will) say, "Of course, as soon as we have set the table!" Your child will be a glutton for all this. You must be the one who sees to it he never overdoes it by always stopping after one session and always keeping your promise to bring the Bits out again later.

It is best to use the morning hours to teach. Afternoon is generally not as good a time but in the evening things start to pick up again. In any event you choose those times when your child is bright and alert and avoid like the plague any time he is not.

Intensity

Great care has been taken by you to insure your Bits are clear and big and mounted with a good-sized border around them. This insures that your child can see the Bits very easily. It means you can show your Bits quickly without worrying whether your child could see them or not. You should position yourself approximately 18″ from your child. It is important that your hands do not obstruct the Bit in any way. The lighting in the area where you teach should be good and you should eliminate visual, auditory, and tactile distractions.

Another aspect of intensity is the intensity of your voice. The younger your child is when you begin, the louder and clearer your voice should be. All mothers intuitively talk to their infants in a voice louder than normal. When you combine this greater intensity with your natural enthusiasm, there is no question your child will "get" the information.

Duration

The speed with which you do each session is astonishingly important to your overall success.

You must present the Bits *very, very, very* quickly.

Even adults, who take in new information *much* more slowly than children do, gain absolutely nothing by staring at a Bit.

This was illustrated clearly during World War II when, due to the astonishing speed at which aircraft then flew (more than 200 miles an hour), it was vital to the lives of front-line soldiers, sailors, marines, and air force people to be able to tell at a glance whether an aircraft was enemy or friendly in order to fire at it or not.

When the military posted up photos of types of aircraft everywhere for the men to study, most service men had difficulty recognizing them. The services quickly learned that the *shorter* length of time they were presented (fractions of a second) the quicker they were identified.

Adults almost always do things too slowly to suit tiny kids. Your motto should be "the faster, the better." You should take one second and no longer per Bit of Intelligence. You should always, always, always show your child a few Bits less than he would really like you to. If you know your kid would love to see fifteen, you show ten; if ten is the maximum your kid could handle at that time, show five.

A smart mother will make a large card for *herself* and pin it up where she can see it briefly many, many times a day until it is emblazoned in her memory. That card will read "Always stop before he wants me to stop!" If you observe that principle you will never abuse your child's precious time and attention.

Your child's attention is superb—make sure you always earn it by very brief, zippy, highly organized, and enthusiastic sessions.

ONE DAY'S SESSIONS

Begin by introducing five different Categories with ten Bits of Intelligence in each. Make sure you teach each Category three times before the day ends. As your confidence grows, begin adding more Categories day by day until you are doing ten different Categories. Again each Category is done for ten seconds three times daily.

ADDING NEW INFORMATION AND RETIRING OLD INFORMATION

Ten days after you have reached ten Categories, begin to retire one old Bit from each Category daily. Place these retired Bits in your file for new use later. Add one new Bit to each Category daily to replace the one you have retired. From this time on you continue to add one new Bit per Category daily or a total of ten new Bits daily. This is a minimum number, *not a maximum.* If you have the ability to introduce new Bits faster, there is no question your child can hold them. The minimum given here is a reflection of time spent searching, cutting, and gluing. It is *not* a reflection of the capacity of the brain of a tiny child. *For all intents and purposes that is without limit.*

When you have run out of Bits in a Category simply retire that Category all together and introduce a whole new Category of ten Bits in its place. Later when you have found enough new Bits on the retired Category you can reintroduce it. Meanwhile file the retired Bits carefully, because you will be needing them later.

THE LIFE-SPAN OF ONE BIT

Every mother should be on top of her child's program. For example—she should know exactly how many times she needs to show her child a new Bit of Intelligence before it becomes old hat to him. It is vital for you to know this because it should be *changing all the time.*

For instance, in the program outlined above, how many times does your child see a Bit before it is retired? If you have followed carefully you will see that the life cycle of one Bit is thirty times, because a new Bit is seen three times daily for ten days. However if you do this program with energy and enthusiasm you will very quickly discover that thirty times over a ten-day period is simply more than is necessary for your child. Why is this? You have been so successful that his visual pathway is now so sophisticated that he needs to see something new only fifteen times over five days. This is a tremendous change in frequency! However it is commonly achieved within a few months of beginning the above program.

You need to ask yourself constantly, "Do I need

to change the life-cycle of this information in recognition of the increased maturity of my child's visual pathway?" If you are enjoying yourself and your child is too, there is no doubt you will one day realize that your child needs to see new information once to know it well. Sometimes for a little while mothers see this as a problem, then they realize they have achieved their objective—a child who can learn anything quickly and effortlessly the first time around. His brain is growing daily and quickly.

But how do you make Bits?

7

how to make bits of intelligence

how to make bits of intelligence

QUALITY

It is not difficult to make very fine quality Bits at home. Indeed the quality must be fine in order for you to use these precious materials with your even more precious child. You should prepare your materials with one thing foremost in your mind—quality. This is not a cute game you will be playing with your child, or icing on the cake. It is his introduction to the knowledge of the world. Your Bits should reflect your respect for what you are going to teach and what your child is going to learn. There is no more precious commodity than knowledge. The only thing worse than something cheap wrapped up in finery is something beyond value made-up cheaply. Your Bits should be regarded as family heirlooms destined to be handed down tenderly from one child to the next, then jealously guarded and saved for the grandchildren.

MATERIALS

You will need the following materials which are usually readily available:

1. Raw Bits of Intelligence
2. Poster board
3. Black "Magic Marker" or other waterproof felt-tipped marker
4. Rubber cement
5. Clear "Contact Paper" or laminate (optional)

Raw Bits of Intelligence

Again you will want raw Bits that are precise, discrete, unambiguous, and new. Your Bits must be precise and new when you get them. However, you may be able to make them discrete and unambiguous after you have found them. In fact you will quickly become quite expert at deciding whether a raw Bit has potential or not. If you have a good potential Bit with a distracting background you must simply cut around the Bit and eliminate the background. If there is a group of objects on the raw Bit cut each out individually and make each into a Bit. If the raw Bit has writing underneath it or around it please cut this away. If the raw Bit has a vague, ambiguous, or misleading title, make sure you have the clearest and most complete label you can find. For example—"beetle" is too general. You need to be specific with "two-spotted ladybird beetle." Lastly, before you throw the leftover material away make sure you have saved and filed any information that came along with that raw Bit. You are going to be needing that information in the future for your child so put it where you can find it easily some months later.

Poster Board

We recommend that Bits be mounted on white, two-sided cardboard. This is sometimes referred to as "poster board," "index board," "illustration boards," et cetera, depending on the composition and quality of the material. Paper does not have adequate rigidity to be used for Bits. A good test for the cardboard you will use is that it should be able to be held in one hand and not "flop." Whatever material you choose should be strong enough to hold up under repeated handling (especially if you plan to have babies beyond those you are currently teaching).

In a situation where white cardboard does not provide adequate contrast with the Bit being prepared, use black poster board or an appropriate color for contrast.

To make your job easier have your cardboard *precut.* If you are buying from a stationery store, art supply store, or paper supply dealer, have them do the work for you with their heavy paper-cutter. Cardboard size should be 11" × 11" (28 cm. × 28 cm.).

Black Waterproof Marker

In order to letter the reverse side of your Bits you will need a wide-tipped black marker. These are marketed under a variety of names, one of the most common being "Magic Marker." This type of marker is waterproof and uses a varnish base ink. Care should be taken to replace the tops of your markers when not in use so that the varnish base does not evaporate. Care should also be taken to keep these tools out of the reach of your child.

Rubber Cement

We have found that rubber cement is the best vehicle for fixing raw Bits to cardboard. A thin coat of rubber cement should be applied to the back of the raw Bit and to the approximate area of the cardboard where the raw Bit will be fixed. When both surfaces are sufficiently dry, press the raw Bit to the cardboard. The bond can be strengthened by placing a clean sheet of paper over your new Bit and rubbing your hand across the surface.

Lamination

The ideal Bit has a clear plastic laminate on both sides. This is ideal because lamination strengthens the Bit making it virtually indestructible, as well as making the Bit impervious to fingerprints and soil. When you consider the time and attention you put into making each Bit, it seems logical that you would wish to preserve it in the best possible way for your future use or the use of others in your family.

Most families cannot afford to have their Bits laminated by machine. However it is possible to purchase wide rolls of clear "Contact Paper" which is a self-adhering material. For anyone wishing to laminate his or her Bits this is an easy material to do it with. This is available in hardware and paint stores that sell kitchen and drawer shelf paper.

PUTTING IT ALL TOGETHER

You have now assembled all the materials that you need to make beautiful Bits. A "production line" should now be set up so that you get the most out of what you have found.

First, you should prepare the raw Bits that you have, being sure that you have the correct identification of the item to be put on the cardboard, and being sure that you have filed any pertinent information about the item.

Second, if the item itself is not *discrete* you must cut out the background so that you have only one item mounted on the cardboard.

Third (and this is a step that is often missed by the novice Bit-maker to her immediate chagrin), label the reverse side of the cardboard *before* mounting the Bit. This will prevent having to throw out the entire thing if you make a mistake while labeling. Proper identification of the item should be neatly lettered on the reverse side using a wide-tipped permanent black marker. Letter size should be *no less than* one inch high—actually, the larger the better.

Next, with your cardboard labeled and your raw Bit prepared, you may now glue it using rubber cement. Care should be taken to use a thin coat of rubber cement, especially if the raw Bit has printing on its reverse side. Generous coats of rubber cement may cause ink to bleed through once the raw Bit is mounted, and this ruins a careful job.

You now have a high-quality, sturdy teaching tool. If you wish to preserve it for many years, you may take the additional step of having your new Bit laminated as described above.

ORGANIZATION

Bits of Intelligence are always organized into Categories. You will find that your Categories start out being very broad. For example—ten typical beginning Categories are "Insects," "Great Inventors," "Countries of the Americas," "Musical Instruments," "Great Art Masterpieces," "Organs of the Body," "Geometric Shapes," "Great Inventions," "Foreign Language Food Words," and "Writers of Children's Literature."

A look at the same program eighteen months later will show a great increase in the sophistication of the organization of Bits. "Insects" are now "wood-boring" or "flying." Rearranging the overall organization of your Bits of Intelligence library will reflect your child's growing ability to connect and relate one Category to another.

Each Category should have a minimum of ten Bits of Intelligence and there is no limit to the number a Category may ultimately have. This depends entirely on availability and your child's interest and enthusiasm for that Category.

When you are finished actively using a Bit of Intelligence you should carefully file it, according to Category, so that you can retrieve it for later use.

SUMMARY

1. Know the definition of Bits of Intelligence.
2. Find a wide variety of raw Bits.
3. Organize Bits into Categories of Intelligence.
4. Cut out raw Bit.
5. Save information about Bits for future Programs of Intelligence.
6. Cut or obtain 11″ × 11″ white poster board.
7. Label 11″ × 11″ card on back with black marker.
8. Put rubber cement on Bit.
9. Mount raw Bit on front of 11″ × 11″ cardboard.
10. Put clear contact paper on both sides of the Bit or laminate both sides.
11. Create a workable filing system for "retired" Bits.

HOW TO FIND BITS OF INTELLIGENCE

The Better Baby Press pioneered and published the first sets of Bits of Intelligence. The Bits of Intelligence Series is constantly being augmented by new Categories. These materials are available from The Better Baby Store and from *Encyclopaedia Britannica*.

In addition to those published Bits, mothers have made literally hundreds of thousands of Bits for their children at home. The best sources for these homemade Bits are books, magazines, maps, posters, teaching cards, and museum cards.

The best type of books are all-color "Treasury of *[subject]*" books. Treasuries of birds, flowers, insects, and mammals are excellent sources for Categories of Bits. Since you want your information in Categories, this type of book provides you with a Category all ready to go. Since the purpose of those books is to instruct and inform, the quality of the illustrations and photographs is generally very good.

Magazines can also be a valuable source for Bits of Intelligence. However, not just any magazine will do. If you are interested in teaching about wildlife, then all the various wildlife magazines will provide you with valuable Bits for this subject.

Maps of countries, states, and continents have proved invaluable for making geography Bits. Since many other Categories can be related to the geography Bits, maps have become a source used by our mothers.

Posters of all kinds have been discovered to provide excellent raw materials for Bits. Government agencies often have posters on regional information that can be made into fine Bits.

Almost all museums offer some good raw materials for Bits. Reproductions of famous artists' works, sculptures, and architecture are readily available. Science museums are also a good potential source for Bits.

There are no limits to the food that can be found for your baby's brain, heart, and soul other than your own ingenuity and the limits of man's knowledge.

Have a joyous time.

8

the organization of knowledge

by Glenn Doman
Janet Doman
Susan Aisen

the organization of
knowledge

The creation by the staff of The Institutes for the
Achievement of Human Potential of the program
for multiplying intelligence of babies has made it
necessary for The Institutes to organize information in a way that is convenient for teaching the baby
or tiny child and is also understandable to the parents who are not necessarily expert in all the fields
of knowledge.

This chapter explains how we have organized information to suit those purposes.

We have begun by dividing all knowledge into ten general *Divisions* and then subdividing them again and again as shown here.

Divisions of Knowledge	(Ten)
Categories	(Many thousands)
Sets	(Tens of thousands)
Bits of Intelligence	(Ten per Set)
Programs of Intelligence	(Ten per Bit)
Magnitudes of Information	(One per Program)

We shall begin with the *Divisions of Knowledge.*

DIVISIONS OF KNOWLEDGE

First:	Biology
Second:	History
Third:	Geography
Fourth:	Music
Fifth:	Art
Sixth:	Mathematics
Seventh:	Human Physiology
Eighth:	General Science
Ninth:	Languages
Tenth:	Literature

Each of these Divisions of Knowledge is further divided into sub-groupings which are called *Categories*.

CATEGORIES

A Category is a collection of *closely related* Bits of Intelligence.

There are thousands of Categories in each Division of Knowledge.

As an example—birds, reptiles, mammals, and fish are all Categories within the Division of Biology.

For the parents' convenience in both teaching and handling materials, the Categories are divided into *Sets* of related Bits of Intelligence.

What precisely is a *Set* and of what is it composed?

SETS

A Set normally contains ten cards each containing a visual Bit of Intelligence on the front and its precise name on the back (ten is a convenient number of 11″ × 11″ cards for mother to handle easily while teaching).

An example of a set would be ten Bits of Intelligence from the Category "Insects":

1. Two-Spotted Ladybird Beetle
2. Giant Walking Stick
3. Dragonfly
4. Housefly
5. Grasshopper
6. Ant
7. Termite
8. Periodical Cicada
9. Monarch Butterfly
10. Bumblebee

A very few Sets contain fewer than ten cards (there are only seven continents; therefore the Category of "Continents" in the Division of Geography has only seven Bits of Intelligence cards).

On the other hand, the Category "States of the United States" would have five Sets each consisting of ten states in order to include all of the fifty states.

Each Set within a Category is therefore composed of ten *Bits of Intelligence* (in rare cases fewer than ten, as has been noted).

Briefly stated, a Bit of Intelligence is defined as follows—

BITS OF INTELLIGENCE

A Bit of Intelligence is a single fact in the form of an illustration, superbly mounted on a piece of high-quality poster board, which is presented visually to a child.

The poster board is 11″ × 11″ in size and is of sufficient stiffness so as not to flop when shown to the child.

The Bit of Intelligence itself, which is mounted on the card, is an extremely accurate drawing, illustration or photograph of the object itself—let us say a reproduction of Leonardo da Vinci's *Mona Lisa.*

This copy must be precise, discrete, and unambiguous.

It must be:

1. Accurate
2. A single item only
3. Specifically named
4. Large (large enough to occupy *most* [but rarely *all*] of the 11″ × 11″ card)
5. Clear

If the Bit of Intelligence is to be part of the family's library to be used not only with new children as they appear in the family but in succeeding generations of the family, it should be laminated with plastic on both sides and should last for generations.

The more splendidly Bits of Intelligence are done, the more effectively will the tiny child learn and the more valuable will the Bit of Intelligence be.

The families which have proven to be the most effective in teaching their children have come to adopt the attitude of the staff of The Institutes regarding the Bits of Intelligence themselves. When these Bits are searched for eagerly, carefully mounted, and carefully preserved by a family they become, in effect, a magnificent library of beautiful and accurate information. They are actually the encyclopedia of the tiny child, the source on which his vast store of future knowledge will be based.

These precious Bits of Intelligence have come to be highly respected by the staff of The Institutes, and subsequently by the parents of The Institutes, as a result of the extremely hard work that first the staff and then the parents have undertaken, to research and produce tens of thousands of Bits of Intelligence.

When the results with the tiny children who had been presented with the Bits of Intelligence became obvious, the respect of the staff and parents for Bits of Intelligence became a sort of reverence.

If reverence seems too strong a word to use to

describe these Bits of Intelligence let us make it clear that we mean reverence in the sense of reverence for splendid books with splendid bindings, reverence for superb paintings such as the *Mona Lisa*, reverence for learning and reverence for truth.

Each Bit of Intelligence has related to it *Programs of Intelligence.*

PROGRAMS OF INTELLIGENCE

A Program of Intelligence is composed of a single fact which is related to a single Bit of Intelligence.

Ten such programs are arranged in a specific order and each is know as a *Magnitude of Information.*

On the next page is a Bit of Intelligence. It is the American Kestrel.

On the reverse side of the page are ten Programs of Intelligence just as they appear on the reverse side of the actual Bit of Intelligence.

MAGNITUDES OF INFORMATION

Each fact is called a Program of Intelligence. These facts are arranged in order of complexity and are then known as Magnitudes of Information. These programs start with facts of the first Magnitude, which are simple, and grow more complex as they ascend in magnitude to the tenth Magnitude, which is the most complex. There are ten for each Bit of Intelligence. These Magnitudes are printed on the back of Bits of Intelligence when ordered through The Institutes or *Encyclopaedia Britannica.* Individual parents may choose to make Bits with or without the programs on the back of the Bits (see the next chapter).

As an example, the America Kestrel is a Bit of Intelligence in the Category of Birds and the Division of Biology.

A fact of the first Magnitude in the Program of Intelligence about the American Kestrel is: "It is commonly called the 'Sparrow Hawk,' but this is a misnomer as it is not a hawk, and eats few sparrows." A fact of the tenth Magnitude is: "The America Kestrel is of the species *Falco sparverius.*"

There are a huge number of relationships between the various Programs of Intelligence within a Category and within a Division. As an example, the fifth, sixth, seventh, eighth, ninth, and tenth Magnitudes in a Program of Intelligence for mammals, birds, reptiles, fish, insects, and amphibians are always phylum (fifth), class (sixth), order (seventh), family (eighth), genus (ninth), and species (tenth).

Thus the child learns that mammals, birds, reptiles, fish, and amphibians are all of the phylum

American Kestrel

1. It is commonly called the "Sparrow Hawk," but this is a misnomer as it is not a hawk, and eats few sparrows.

2. It eats mainly insects and small mammals.

3. This bird adapts well to the desert, as it tolerates heat well and needs little water.

4. The species has been used successfully in falconry.

5. It likes nesting in holes in trees, cacti and high cliffs.

6. Class: Aves

7. Order: Falconiformes

8. Family: Falconidae

9. Genus: Falco

0. Species: Falco sparverius

Illustration by Roslynn Middleman Mansfield

Vertebrata while insects are of the phylum *Arthropoda.* Thus the tiny child learns scientific classifications of creatures while learning facts of like magnitude. He is totally unaware that he is doing so. He thinks he is having a great time with his mother—and indeed he is. He is also learning Linnean Classification which very few adults ever learn.

A LIST OF CATEGORIES

This section lists ten Categories in each of the ten Divisions of Knowledge for a total of one hundred Categories. Obviously the parent using these one hundred examples could easily think of another hundred or even a thousand with minimum effort. These are therefore listed as examples.

Division: **Biology**

Category:
1. Mammals
2. Birds
3. Reptiles
4. Amphibians
5. Fish
6. Shells and Shellfish
7. Insects
8. Flowers
9. Trees
10. Plants and Shrubs

Division:	**History**
Category:	1. Great Leaders
	2. Great Inventors
	3. Great Scientists
	4. Great Explorers
	5. Presidents of the United States
	6. Famous Battles
	7. Monarchs of Great Britain
	8. American Indians
	9. Founding Fathers of the United States
	10. Prehistoric Man

Division: ***Geography***

Category:
1. Continents and Oceans
2. Countries of the Americas
3. Countries of Europe
4. Countries of Africa
5. Countries of Asia
6. States of the United States
7. The Flags of the World
8. Traffic Signs and Symbols (U.S.)
9. Mountains
10. Great Rivers of the World

Division:	**Music**
Category:	1. Musical Instruments
	2. Musical Notes
	3. Musical Symbols
	4. Great Composers
	5. Musical Intervals
	6. Musical Chords
	7. Great Singers
	8. Great Performers
	9. Ancient Musical Instruments
	10. Musical Phrases

Division: **Art**

Category: 1. Great Artists
 2. Masterpieces of Van Gogh
 3. Masterpieces of Picasso
 4. Masterpieces of da Vinci
 5. Masterpieces of Cezanne
 6. Masterpieces of Rembrandt
 7. Masterpieces of Michelangelo
 8. Masterpieces of Dürer
 9. Masterpieces of Botticelli
 10. Masterpieces of Holbein

Division: **Mathematics**

Category:
1. Geometric Shapes
2. Angles
3. Measurement and Calculation Tools
4. Mathematical Symbols
5. Geometric Solids
6. Roman Numerals
7. Metric Measurements
8. Great Mathematicians
9. Coordinate Geometry
10. Dot Cards (True Numbers)

Division: **Physiology**

Category:
1. Organs of the Body
2. Bones of the Body
3. Muscles of the Body
4. Parts of a Cell
5. Digestive System
6. Circulatory System
7. Teeth
8. Nervous System
9. Reproductive System (Female)
10. Reproductive System (Male)

Division: **General Science**

Category:
1. Planets
2. Constellations
3. Chemical Elements
4. Minerals
5. Automobiles
6. Trains
7. Airplanes
8. Ships
9. Inventions
10. Tools

Division: **Languages**

Category: 1. Food
                     2. Household Objects
                     3. Animals
                     4. Nature
                     5. Actions
                     6. Antonyms
                     7. Clothing
                     8. Family Members
                     9. Vehicles
                     10. Things Around the
                         Neighborhood

Division:	**Literature**
Category:	1. Authors of Children's Classic Books
	2. Writers of Children's Literature
	3. American Authors
	4. American Poets
	5. Shakespearean Characters
	6. English Authors
	7. English Poets
	8. Great Performers
	9. Great Philosophers
	10. Poets of the World

We have therefore listed one hundred Categories of knowledge.

If each of these Categories were made up of a single Set we would now have 1,000 Bits of Intelligence (since each Set is made up of ten related Bits of Intelligence). An example of a Set is given on page *144*.

Since each Bit has related to it a Program of Intelligence of which there are ten (the ten Magnitudes) concerning that single Bit, we would now be dealing with *ten thousand* facts. Counting the Bit itself there would actually be *eleven thousand*.

In light of the great importance of this huge amount of knowledge which has been derived from only a single Set from each of a hundred Categories, it seems wise to give a number of specific examples of how Programs of Intelligence are created as well as *general examples* of how Magnitudes of Information are determined.

9

the creation of programs of intelligence

by Janet Doman
Susan Aisen

the creation of programs of intelligence

Once you have established a broad network of Bits of Intelligence systematically arranged in Categories it is time to expand your intelligence program.

When you have taught your child one thousand Bits of Intelligence, you should start creating Programs of Intelligence.

While a Category of Intelligence establishes breadth of knowledge in an area, Programs of Intelligence provide an ascending Magnitude of knowledge within a Category. Each new Program within a Category adds a higher Magnitude, starting with the most simple information and ending with the most profound. Here is an example:

Division:	Biology
Category:	Insects
Bit of Intelligence:	Periodical Cicada
1st Magnitude:	Periodical Cicada spend most of their lives underground.
2nd Magnitude	They spend their lives underground in an immature form, without wings.
3rd Magnitude:	When they come above ground, they shed their old skins and emerge as adult, winged insects.
4th Magnitude:	After living thirteen to seventeen years underground, they live only a few weeks aboveground.

5th Magnitude:	The Periodical Cicada is of the phylum *Arthropoda.*
6th Magnitude:	The Periodical Cicada is of the class *Insecta.*
7th Magnitude:	The Periodical Cicada is of the order *Hemiptera.*
8th Magnitude:	The Periodical Cicada is of the family *Cicadidae.*
9th Magnitude:	The Periodical Cicada is of the genus *Magicicada.*
10th Magnitude:	The Periodical Cicada is of the species, *Magicicada Septendecim.*

Imagine two-year-olds knowing thousands of Bits and understanding Linnaen classification!

Old Carolus Linnaeus (1707–1778) who first brought the order of scientific classification to the world of biology would, I believe, be delighted to know that hundreds of two-year-olds (which may *already* be thousands and which tomorrow will be tens of thousands) know and understand the work he pioneered. It would warm the cockles of his Swedish heart. Very, very, very few grownups have more than the foggiest notion that phylum, class, order, family, genus, and species exist, never mind what the crow *is* in each of those classifications.

Most little kids are delighted to know that the ferocious grizzly bear's proper scientific name is *Ursus Horribilis.* Especially do they love it when Mom or Dad makes a properly horrible grizzly bear face and pronounces the name with proper dread in the voice when teaching the tenth Magnitude Program on the Bit, "Grizzly Bear," by announcing that the grizzly bear is of the species *URSUS HORRIBILIS!!!*

Clearly these Magnitudes go on and on and are limited only by man's present state of knowledge in any one area.

When you begin Programs of Intelligence, your objective should be to establish *breadth of knowledge* across one and all of your Categories, rather than completing the *degree of magnitude* of any individual Bit or Category. Initially you should aim to do a Program of Intelligence of the first Magnitude on every retired Bit in all your Categories. As you complete this step you begin to build to higher and higher Magnitudes in *all* of the Categories.

As this is accomplished at ascending Magnitudes, information about Bits within a Category begins to overlap. Then Categories themselves become interrelated. In the end your Program becomes a vast network of knowledge in which no new piece of information is added without shedding light on some other piece of information.

When you have reached this stage you will find the more you teach your child the more he will be able to hold.

This is a very nice state of affairs for him and for you.

OTHER CHARACTERISTICS OF PROGRAMS OF INTELLIGENCE

1. *A Program of Intelligence is accurate.* It is a fact, not an opinion or an assumption. For example, "George Washington was the first president of the United States" is a Program of Intelligence.

   "Zachary Taylor was a bad president" is *not* a Program of Intelligence—it's an opinion.

2. *A Program of Intelligence is clear.* It is worded as clearly and directly as possible so it is not open to misinterpretation of any kind. For example, "The cheetah is the fastest mammal on earth" is a clear statement that cannot be misinterpreted.

Programs of Intelligence may be used to relate one retired category of Bits to another retired category. For example, "George Washington was born in Virginia," for the child who knows George Washington and the state of Virginia, is a nice neat way of tying two seemingly unrelated Categories together. As you and your child discover more ways to relate one Category to another, your excitement in discovering the next new relationship will really be intensified.

Programs of Intelligence should be familiar. It is quite true that "Bach was called the master of the fugue" but as a first Program about Bach it is probably a bit esoteric. "Bach had twenty-three children" will get you where you want to go better and faster. You can easily come back and give Programs of greater magnitude about a man who had twenty-three children. In short you want initial Magnitudes to open doors for your child. In order for them to want to peek behind those doors, the initial Programs need to relate to that with which they are already familiar. You may then cover quite unfamiliar grounds without any difficulty.

Programs of Intelligence should be *interesting*. It is a fact that Philadelphia is "x" square miles but this is dry stuff unless you are doing mathematical programs and are headed somewhere with square miles. How much more interesting to know that "Philadelphia is the home of the Liberty Bell" (or

". . . home of The Institutes"). If a fact you have found looks dry and dull to you, the chances are good it will look dry and dull to your child. Go for the things that excite your interest, and you will get your child's interest.

Programs of Intelligence should be amusing where it is appropriate. Humor is the most under-valued, underrated, underestimated teaching device which exists. Few Programs of Intelligence made a bigger hit with The Evan Thomas Institute kids than "Tchaikovsky held his chin with his left hand while he conducted with his right hand because he was afraid his head would fall off." The world is full of amusing facts—use them.

HOW TO FIND PROGRAMS OF INTELLIGENCE

The first place to gather information about a retired Bit is the source where you found the Bit in the first place. Some wise parents photocopy information on the backs of their Bits before mounting them and file the information. You will also need either a full encyclopedia (*Encyclopaedia Britannica* is a splendid one) or a good one-volume encyclopedia. Comprehensive dictionaries are also very helpful to every aspect of your Program. If you can't afford to buy one, spend time at your local library.

When in doubt, look it up. Don't give your child what you *think* is the truth. Check your facts as accurately as you possibly can.

HOW TO PREPARE PROGRAMS OF INTELLIGENCE

There are four basic ways to present Programs of Intelligence. The easiest is to write the Programs you are planning to teach on 5″ × 7″ index cards. Put five Programs on each card. (You will be reading them to your child.)

Another way of teaching a Program is to write out the Program on sentence cards. You will also be reading them to him, the difference being that he will be able to see the words as you read them out.

Yet another way to introduce Programs is to make a very nice homemade reading book with one Program per page, five to ten Programs per book. This is read by you to your child and later by your child to himself. Of course the size of print used is based on your child's reading level at that moment.

The fourth way to present Programs of Intelligence is to have them carefully printed on the back of each Bit of Intelligence in ascending order of magnitude from first Magnitude at the top of the card (immediately under the name of the Bit) to the tenth Magnitude at the bottom. These can be made up by the parent when the original Bit was made or can be gotten already made up.

HOW TO TEACH PROGRAMS OF INTELLIGENCE

One Session

One session should consist of no more than five Programs (one Program for each of five Bits). Programs take longer to read aloud than Bits and, in order to keep sessions brief, it is necessary to do fewer of them.

If you are simply telling your child the Programs, use an index card system to keep you straight. It is fun to dig out the five old Bits and show them quickly as you give your child some new information.

For example—you pull retired Bits of Insects and say as you show,

Two-Spotted Ladybird Beetle—"The Two-Spotted Ladybird Beetle eats other insects, many of which are pests to humans."

Giant Walking Stick—"If its protective mimicry fails, the Giant Walking Stick can excrete a foulsmelling liquid to ward off predators."

Dragonfly—"The nymph stage of this insect lives underwater, eating tadpoles, small fish, and aquatic insects."

Housefly—"Adult Houseflies feed mainly on liquids that contain either sweet or decaying substances."

Grasshopper—"The Grasshopper subsists on grasses, crop plants, and fruits."

This should take about 10–15 seconds. If you prefer to use written-out sentences instead of showing the actual Bit, you show the sentence as you read it.

If you prefer the book, you sit down and read it with your child. Whichever way you decide to use it should be fast and must be fun.

One Day's Sessions

It is fun to use five different Categories of five Programs each to begin with. Do each Category three times in the day. You can expand this to include as many Categories as you wish.

ADDING NEW PROGRAMS
AND RETIRING OLD ONES

After five days retire all the Programs you have been using, and put in five new Programs in each Category. This means a new Program will be done three times over five days to total fifteen times before being retired. You will be adding at least twenty-five new Programs every five days. If you see your child is learning his Programs more quickly, retire them sooner and introduce new ones.

When you run out of good Programs in a particular Category retire the Category and begin working on another retired Category.

MAGNITUDES OF INFORMATION

When you have done many Programs of the first Magnitude you begin to teach Programs of the second Magnitude. Each Magnitude requires a broader general knowledge than the one before it. Therefore your first Programs will contain new information but in a familiar context. You will use familiar vocabulary in initial Programs. As you advance, your use of vocabulary becomes more and more sophisticated. In this way your child is always reaching above his head for new information while at the same time standing on a very firm foundation of understanding. It is up to you to make each step upward a combination of new information clothed in a context he can readily understand and appreciate.

Indeed, the correct balance of these two elements is the foundation of all fine teaching.

SUMMARY

By this point it should be clear to you that you can teach your child virtually anything that you can present in an honest and factual way. All the subjects that you know and love you can offer to your tiny child. All the subjects that you were interested in learning about but never had the opportunity to do you can now teach your child. Even those subjects with which you may have had difficulty now begin to be a possibility.

Indeed, mothers who have been teaching Bits of Intelligence to their children for twelve months or more find that their attitude toward knowledge and learning is completely changed. For such mothers the world is their oyster. There is no subject that is too formidable for them. They may not *know* every Bit in the world, but they have a very good idea of where to *get* every Bit. They have the world wired.

We are continually amazed at the endless imagination of our professional mothers and fathers. It is safe to say that no two mothers ever did the same Intelligence Program. Each child's Program is a unique reflection of the creativity, imagination, and inventiveness of his mother. Like the ability of the tiny child, the inventiveness of a professional mother appears to be limitless.

Every mother who embarks upon this adventure expects to expand her tiny child's ability. She does this with such vim and vigor that she hardly takes the time to assess the changes that are taking place in her own abilities and viewpoint, until one day when she finds herself happily preparing to teach her child calculus or nuclear physics and is brought up short by her own bravado. She is startled, but not for long.

"I always secretly knew I could learn anything," she says to herself and gets back to work teaching her child.

We are no longer able to learn at even a good fraction of the speed of a tiny child, nor is the quality of our learning even comparable with his. However we have the thrill and the honor of taking this superb learner and gently lifting him onto our shoulders. What broad shoulders our professional parents have and what a panoramic view they provide for our tiny kids.

10

how to make programs of intelligence

by Glenn Doman
Janet Doman
Susan Aisen

how to make programs
of intelligence

While The Institutes themselves, and all publishers whose materials (Bits, Categories, Programs) receive The Institutes' Signet of Certification, follow the guidelines with a high degree of exactness the individual parent may choose to set up some other orderly system of presenting Programs and Magnitudes of Information. The systems used by The Institutes and presented here have the virtue of having been tried and used successfully over and over again with babies and tiny kids for many years.

We have learned that it is wise, when creating Programs of Intelligence, to use the most authoritative sources available as reference material. The local public library is a first-rate source if a family's personal library does not contain an authoritative work on the subject to be taught.

If the subject to be taught were a Program of Intelligence on the Eastern Bluebird,

Division	Biology
Category	Birds
Set	Song Birds of the East
Bit of Intelligence	Eastern Bluebird

then the authority used to write a Program of Intelligence might be Roger Tory Peterson's splendid and very popular *A Field Guide to the Birds: Eastern Land and Water Birds* (Boston: Houghton, Mifflin, 1947.)

If you are one of the innumerable families who already own this wonderful book you would quickly find that the Eastern Bluebird is from

the Phylum	Vertebrata
the Class	Aves
the Order	Passeriformes
the Family	Turdidae
the Genus	Sialia
the Species	Sialis

This would give you the fifth, sixth, seventh, eighth, ninth, and tenth Magnitudes of Information in the Program of Intelligence concerning the Eastern Bluebird.

The first Magnitude might be: "The Eastern Bluebird looks round-shouldered when perched." (This is both true and rather amusing to children and therefore a first-rate beginning.)

The second Magnitude might be: "The Eastern Bluebird is a bit larger than an English Sparrow—seven inches (18 cm.)."

The third Magnitude might be: "The Eastern Bluebird is a blue bird with a rusty red breast."

The fourth Magnitude might be: "The Eastern Bluebird's voice says 'chur-wi' or 'tru-ly.' "

You would therefore have a splendid Program of Intelligence from a single source.

If your family is fortunate enough to own a first-class encyclopedia such as the patriarch of all encyclopedias, the much-respected *Encyclopaedia Britannica,* then all the information necessary to make virtually endless Programs of Intelligence is already at its members' fingertips.

The *Encyclopaedia Britannica* contains twelve billion, five hundred million bits of information and will therefore hold you for quite a while.

Let's consider some more Programs of Intelligence and how they are created.

Let's try the Program of Intelligence for the Bit of Intelligence, "Wolf"—

Division	Biology
Category	Mammals
Set	Predators
Bit of Intelligence	Wolf

Remember that the first four Magnitudes—those most likely to be given to very young children—should be as interesting and as much fun for you and your child as you can possibly make them.

PROGRAM OF INTELLIGENCE

THE WOLF

1. A wolf is a wild dog which lives in wilderness areas of North America, Greenland, Europe, and Asia.
2. Wolves hunt deer, moose, caribou, and elk for food.
3. Wolves can trot over forty miles in a day.
4. Wolves are highly intelligent and man is virtually their only enemy.

5. Wolves are of the phylum *Vertebrata.*
6. Wolves are of the class *Mammalia.*
7. Wolves are of the order *Carnivora.*
8. Wolves are of the family *Canidae.*
9. Wolves are of the genus *Canus.*
10. Wolves are of the species *Lupus.*

FORMULA FOR THE CREATION OF PREDATOR MAGNITUDES

1. Where do they live? (Simple and if possible amusing to a tiny child.)
2. What do they eat?
3. What is an outstanding characteristic?
4. What is the number-one enemy of these animals?
5. What is the phylum of these animals?
6. What is the class of these animals?
7. What is the order of these animals?
8. What is the family of these animals?
9. What is the genus of these animals?
10. What is the species of these animals?

Now let's look at the Program of Intelligence for the Bit of Intelligence, "Thomas Jefferson"—

Division	History
Category	Presidents of the United States

| Set | The First Ten Presidents |
| Bit of Intelligence | Thomas Jefferson |

PROGRAM OF INTELLIGENCE

THOMAS JEFFERSON

1. Thomas Jefferson was born in Virginia.
2. Thomas Jefferson played the violin as a young boy and as a grown man.
3. Thomas Jefferson was the third president of the United States.
4. Thomas Jefferson wrote most of the Declaration of Independence.
5. Thomas Jefferson did not fight as a soldier in the Revolutionary War.
6. Thomas Jefferson was the governor of Virginia.
7. Thomas Jefferson founded the Democratic Party.
8. During Thomas Jefferson's presidency, the United States doubled its size by gaining the land from the Mississippi River to the Rocky Mountains.
9. Thomas Jefferson's home was called "Monticello."

10. Thomas Jefferson and John Adams died on the same day, fifty years after the signing of the Declaration of Independence.

FORMULA FOR CREATION OF PRESIDENTS' MAGNITUDES

1. The state where the president was born.
2. A fact about the president's youth.
3. The number of this president of the United States.
4. The most significant contribution of this person.
5. A fact about his participation in politics or historical events.
6. A fact about the political positions he held.
7. A fact about his contribution to politics or historical events.
8. His major accomplishment during his presidency.
9. The president's home or memorial site.
10. The date or circumstances of the president's death.

Now let's try the Program of Intelligence for the Bit of Intelligence, "Pennsylvania"

Division	Geography
Category	States of the United States
Set	Eastern States
Bit of Intelligence	Pennsylvania

PROGRAM OF INTELLIGENCE

PENNSYLVANIA

1. The largest chocolate factory in the world is at Hershey, Pennsylvania.
2. Pennsylvania is in the eastern part of the United States.
3. The capital city of Pennsylvania is Harrisburg.
4. All the hard coal, or anthracite, in the United States comes from Pennsylvania.
5. The state bird of Pennsylvania is the Ruffed Grouse.
6. The state flower of Pennsylvania is the Mountain Laurel.
7. King Charles II of England granted to William Penn the land which is now Pennsylvania.
8. The word "Pennsylvania" means Penn's Woods.
9. The Declaration of Independence of the

United States was adopted by the Second Continental Congress in Philadelphia, Pennsylvania, on July 4, 1776.

10. Pennsylvania was the second state to join the United States of America.

FORMULA FOR THE CREATION OF STATES' MAGNITUDES

1. An interesting or significant fact about the state's industrial or agricultural contribution.
2. The geographical location of the state.
3. The capital city.
4. The state's most significant natural resource.
5. The state bird.
6. The state flower.
7. How the state land was acquired.
8. How the state was named.
9. The most significant historical or political fact about the state.
10. The order of the state to join the Union.

Let's see what a Program of Intelligence for the Bit of Intelligence "Violin" might look like—

Division   Music
Category   Musical Instruments

Set   Stringed Instruments
Bit of Intelligence   Violin

PROGRAM OF INTELLIGENCE

VIOLIN

1. The violin is a stringed instrument.
2. The violin has four strings (E, A, D, and G).
3. The violin is played with a bow.
4. The bow of a violin is strung with horsehair which, when drawn across the instrument's strings, causes them to vibrate.
5. Parts of the violin include the tuning pegs, the tailpiece, and the soundpost.
6. The strings of the violin are connected to the tuning pegs at the top end and to a tailpiece at the bottom end.
7. The violin was first made in Italy in the sixteenth century.
8. The first violins were used to play dance music.
9. Claudio Monteverdi included the violin in the orchestra of an opera for the first time.
10. Today, thirty-five violins play in the modern full symphony orchestra which is a greater number than any other instrument.

FORMULA FOR THE CREATION OF MUSICAL INSTRUMENT MAGNITUDES

1. Type of instrument.
2. Specific information about the type of instrument.
3. How is the instrument played?
4. Specific information about how the instrument is played.
5. List some parts of the instrument.
6. Specific information about a part of the instrument.
7. Where did the instrument originate?
8. What was the instrument's first role?
9. A further role of the instrument (may be associated with a famous figure in music).
10. The modern role of the instrument (in the orchestra or in some other area).

How may we present the Program of Intelligence for the Bit of Intelligence *The Last Supper* by Leonardo da Vinci?

Division	Art
Category	Great Art
	Masterpieces

Set	Great Art Masterpieces of da Vinci
Bit of Intelligence	*The Last Supper*

PROGRAM OF INTELLIGENCE

THE LAST SUPPER

1. *The Last Supper* was painted by Leonardo da Vinci.
2. *The Last Supper* was painted in Milan, Italy.
3. *The Last Supper* is a mural, which is a painting on a wall.
4. The figure of Jesus Christ is in the center of the mural.
5. The twelve men around Jesus are his students who are called "disciples" or "apostles."
6. *The Last Supper* took Leonardo three years to complete.
7. The fresco technique, which is painting on wet plaster, was used in the creation of this work.
8. Soon after Leonardo completed the mural the paint began to flake away and today *The Last Supper* is in poor condition.

9. *The Last Supper* exists today in the Convent of Santa Maria delle Grazie in Milan.
10. The artist Leonardo also studied anatomy, astronomy, botany, and geology; he designed machines and originated other inventions.

FORMULA FOR THE CREATION OF
ART MAGNITUDES

1. Name of the artist who created the work.
2. Where was the work done?
3. What type of work is it?
4. The subject of the work.
5. Some of the details of the work.
6. When was the work done and/or how long did it take to complete?
7. What technique was used?
8. An anecdote about the work.
9. Where is the work today?
10. Some information about the artist.

How about the Program of Intelligence for the Bit of Intelligence, "Rectangle"?

Division   Mathematics
Category   Geometric Shapes

Set   Sided Shapes

Bit of Intelligence   Rectangle

PROGRAM OF INTELLIGENCE

SIDED SHAPES

1. A rectangle has four sides.
2. A rectangle has four inside angles.
3. The rectangle has two pairs of equal opposite sides.
4. Each one of the interior angles of a rectangle is called a "right angle."
5. A rectangle is defined as a parallelogram with four equal angles.
6. The sum of all the interior angles of a rectangle is 360°.
7. Rectangles are two-dimensional figures.
8. Rectangles are studied in the branch of geometry called plane geometry.
9. In plane geometry a rectangle is classified as a type of convex quadrilateral.
10. The word rectangle comes from the Latin words *rectus,* meaning "right" and *angulus,* meaning "angle," describing the four interior right angles of the rectangle.

FORMULA FOR THE CREATION OF
SIDED SHAPE MAGNITUDES

1. How many sides does it have?
2. How many inside angles does it have?
3. A characteristic of its sides.
4. What are its inside angles?
5. What is its definition?
6. What is the sum of all its interior angles?
7. State that it is a two-dimensional figure.
8. State that it is studied in plane geometry.
9. In plane geometry how is the shape classified?
10. What is the root of the name of the shape?

Here's a method of creating a Program of Intelligence on the Bit of Intelligence, "The Heart"—

Division	Human Physiology
Category	Organs of the Body
Set	Organs of the Upper Body
Bit of Intelligence	The Heart

PROGRAM OF INTELLIGENCE

THE HEART

1. The heart pumps blood to all parts of the body.
2. The heart is the size of the fist and weighs less than one pound.
3. The heart lies between the lungs slightly to the left of the sternum.
4. The heart is a muscle that stretches and tightens to move.
5. Tubes called "veins" bring blood to the heart and tubes called "arteries" carry blood away from the heart.
6. There are four chambers of the heart—two atria and two ventricles.
7. The atria of the heart collect blood from the veins.
8. The ventricles of the heart pump blood through the arteries to other areas of the body.
9. Blood is pumped to the lungs by the heart so oxygen can be added before it is pumped to the body.
10. The medical name for heart is "the cardiac organ."

FORMULA FOR THE CREATION OF
BODY ORGAN MAGNITUDES

1. The function of the organ.
2. The size and weight of the organ.
3. The location of the organ in the body.
4. How the organ works.
5. Parts of the body that are related to the organ.
6. Specific parts of the organ itself.
7. Specific parts of the organ described by function.
8. Specific parts of the organ described by function.
9. The organ's relationship to other organs.
10. The medical name for the organ or a fact about the medical name.

Let's try an example of the Program of Intelligence for the Bit of Intelligence, "Mars"—

Division	General Science
Category	Planets
Set	Planets of the Solar System
Bit of Intelligence	Mars

PROGRAM OF INTELLIGENCE

MARS

1. Mars is reddish in color.
2. Mars is the fourth closest planet to the sun.
3. Mars' size is a little over half that of Earth.
4. Life forms from Earth could not live on Mars because it is too cold and there is almost no water and very little oxygen.
5. Mars is named for the Roman god of war.
6. The average temperature on Mars is 80° below zero.
7. Mars takes 687 days to travel once around the sun.
8. On July 20, 1976, the unmanned U.S. spacecraft, "Viking I," landed on Mars and sent back close-up photographs from Mars to Earth.
9. An 100 pound object on Earth would weigh 38 pounds on Mars.
10. The force of gravity on Mars is ⅜ths as strong as on Earth.

FORMULA FOR THE CREATION OF PLANET MAGNITUDES

1. Appearance of the planet from Earth.
2. The order of the planet from the sun.
3. The size of the planet compared to Earth.
4. Conditions on the planet.
5. The origin of the planet's name.
6. The temperature on the planet's surface.
7. The length of time it takes the planet to complete one orbit of the sun.
8. What exploration of this planet has occurred?
9. How much would an object weigh on this planet compared to its weight on Earth?
10. What is the force of gravity on this planet compared to Earth's gravity?

It's easy to do things from literature because so many people are involved. Let's take a Program of Intelligence for the Bit of Intelligence, "Shakespeare."

Division	Literature
Category	English Poets
Set	Poems of Shakespeare
Bit of Intelligence	William Shakespeare

PROGRAM OF INTELLIGENCE

WILLIAM SHAKESPEARE

1. William Shakespeare was a poet.
2. William Shakespeare was born in England.
3. William Shakespeare came from a prosperous family who lived in Stratford-Upon-Avon.
4. William Shakespeare married Anne Hathaway when he was eighteen years old.
5. William Shakespeare moved to London with his wife and three children when he was about twenty-eight years old.
6. The first work of Shakespeare to be published was the poem "Venus and Adonis," which appeared when he was twenty-nine years old.
7. Shakespeare wrote comic plays, tragic plays, and historical plays.
8. Many of Shakespeare's plays were presented at the Globe Theatre in London.
9. Shakespeare became the best-known poet in England.
10. Shakespeare is considered by many people to be the greatest playwright who ever lived.

FORMULA FOR THE CREATION OF ENGLISH POET MAGNITUDES

1. What was the person?
2. Where and when was the person born?
3. In what kind of environment was the person raised?
4. Did the person have a family and who were they?
5. Where did the person spend most of his life?
6. When was the first major work done by this person and what was it?
7. What was the scope of his work?
8. Where were the person's works presented or where are they today?
9. How was the person regarded by his contemporaries?
10. What is a good overall generalization of the accomplishments of the person?

Finally we shall demonstrate how to create a Program of Intelligence for the Bit of Intelligence word "Animals" in the Japanese language:

Division	Language
Category	Japanese
Set	Japanese Words
Bit of Intelligence	"Animals"

PROGRAM OF INTELLIGENCE

JAPANESE WORD ''ANIMALS''

	Written Form	Romanji	English
1.	犬	inu	dog
2.	猫	neko	cat
3.	兎	usagi	rabbit
4.	馬	uma	horse
5.	豚	buta	pig
6.	蛇	hebi	snake
7.	猿	saru	monkey
8.	象	zo	elephant
9.	鰐	wani	alligator
10.	パンダ	panda	panda

FORMULA FOR THE CREATION OF
JAPANESE WORD MAGNITUDES

1. Most popular animal.
2. Second most popular animal.
3. Third popular animal.
4. Fourth most popular animal.
5. Fifth most popular animal.
6. Sixth most popular animal.

7. Seventh most popular animal.
8. Eighth most popular animal.
9. Ninth most popular animal.
10. An uncommon but popular animal.

In Chapter 8 we listed for you ten Categories from each Division.

Since there are ten Divisions, that makes a total of 100 Categories.

Now obviously, using merely the Categories we have already listed, a parent could create one thousand Bits of Intelligence.

It is also obvious that preparing ten Programs of Intelligence for each Bit of Intelligence, so as to create ten Magnitudes of Intelligence for each Bit would result in ten thousand Programs of Intelligence.

Or a total of ten thousand facts.

Yet clearly we shall only have scratched the surface.

"The world is so full of a number of things I am sure we should all be as happy as kings" (and as busy as beavers making up the endless Bits of Intelligence which are possible).

Having indicated the manner in which Divisions

are divided into Categories, Categories into Sets, Sets into Bits, and Bits into Programs thus creating Magnitudes, we would like to point out that there are *many* advantages in using and maintaining this method of organization of knowledge. Among these advantages are:

1. The ability to trade Sets with neighbors thus doubling, tripling, or quadrupling the number of Bits of Intelligence available to your child with no increase in the time you spend in manufacturing them.
2. The ability to add to your own Sets by purchases of already prepared Sets from The Institutes' bookstore or from *Encyclopaedia Britannica.*

SUMMARY

Parents can deal with the Programs of Intelligence in a number of different ways.

Parents may make cards upon which they have written out ten Programs of Intelligence of the first Magnitude for a single Set of Bits from which they will teach the baby.

If this is the case, then obviously the parents will then prepare ten Programs of Intelligence of the second Magnitude, and so on, until they have reached Programs of Intelligence of the tenth Magnitude, for a total of a hundred Programs per Set of Bits.

Or,

The parents may wish instead to prepare a hundred sentence cards (one for each Program of a Set), with the printing large enough for their particular tiny child to read it. Having done so, they can have the child learn each Program by reading each Program as it is presented by Mom or Dad.

Or,

The parents may put the ten Programs of Intelligence which compose the ten Magnitudes of that Bit into a single homemade book for the baby to read, entitled "George Washington" or "The Wolf" or "The Blue Jay."

Or,

The parents (after having taught the first thousand Bits, which probably did not have the ten Programs on the back of each card) may wish to hereafter put the Programs on the back of each Bit so as to include the entire ten Magnitudes for each Bit.

If so, the parents should print each Program of the ten Magnitudes on the back of the Bit, neatly and legibly, before they are plasticized. Remember that these precious Bits are going to become family heirlooms and deserve to be treated with great respect.

Since all of The Institutes' Bits now contain ten Magnitudes of Information on the back of each Bit in every Set, The Institutes' staff is now aware, as are all the parents who have researched and laid out Programs of Intelligence, of the many hours of research and dollar cost required to make a full set with a hundred programs.

The approximate cost to find an appropriate set of ten related Bits and then to research one hundred Programs of Intelligence to provide the ten Magnitudes required for each Bit, then to prepare the Bit, then to carefully print the hundred Programs on the back of the Set, then to plasticize each of the cards, cost the parents a minimum amount of $10.00 per set and a maximum of $44.00 per set, with most sets requiring an average of about $13.00 in cash outlay.

The amount of *time* required for preparing a Set

of Bits, including research and preparation of materials, varies from about three hours per Set to about fifteen hours per Set, depending upon the subject and the parents' access to research material such as *Encyclopaedia Britannica.*

This means that (as we said earlier), the average set, in terms of materials, cost the parents $13.00 in cash outlay, to which must be added an average time of about nine hours per Set for first-rate research, physical preparation of the Bit on one side and Programs on the reverse, followed by proper plasticizing costs (counting the parents' time at minimal wages)—totaling about $29.25.

This would mean a total cost of $42.25 if the mother charged her time to the project, but average cost of $13.00 if she charged only her cost of the materials.

If parents are going to invest that much time and money in materials, they should be very careful to make that material superbly and to preserve it in such a way that it lasts for generations.

There is nothing to compare with personally finding Bits, researching for Programs, and putting the materials together into a beautiful set of Bits to give one a vast respect for what goes into a single superb Bit, reverence for the subject being taught, respect for it as a family heritage, and a capacity for shuddering in horror when someone refers to it as a "flash card."

It was in desperation that thousands of parents turned to The Institutes to plead that The Institutes publish its own huge and truly unique library of Bits, Sets, Programs, and Magnitudes of Information and make them available to parents.

The parents were delighted when The Institutes agreed. New sets are being published which are of the highest quality, as quickly as The Institutes' finances make that possible.

The Institutes have also permitted *Encyclopaedia Britannica*, which publishes several of The Institutes' programs, to publish Bits in an identical way, bearing The Institutes' Signet of Certification.

How these Sets of Bits with Programs of Intelligence can be obtained is included in the final pages of this book.

While, as we have just pointed out, it is highly advantageous to adhere to The Institutes' method of organizing knowledge, *parents should feel not the slightest reluctance to use their own splendid imaginations to design Sets and Bits of Intelligence as well as to create Magnitudes of Information.*

The staff of The Institutes have learned a very great deal from the ingenuity of parents in creating and designing Sets of Intelligence from their own backgrounds and abilities. These have ranged from plumber's tools to the atomic structure of chemical elements. Children have delighted in them and have vastly broadened their knowledge and grown their brains by such material.

Feel free to use your own imagination within the advantageous structure of knowledge upon which The Institutes have spent so many years.

If the reader has been playing close attention, she will by now be aware that she has in her possession (in this chapter) one hundred Programs of Intelligence which have already *been* researched for her. Figuring her time at minimum wages she has just saved herself roughly three hundred dollars of time, which is a good deal more than she paid for the book.

Isn't that nice?

11

millions of connections
in thirty seconds

by Glenn Doman

millions of connections
in thirty seconds

The Evan Thomas Institute, which has within it the Early Development Program and The International School, both On Campus and Off Campus, is named for Dr. Evan Welling Thomas, one of the greatest human beings of all times. Dr. Thomas was the Medical Director of The Children's Evaluation Institute of The Institutes.

Dr. Thomas died holding a brain-injured child in his arms, in his 84th year of life.

Evan Thomas, in addition to being brilliant, was without question the least-complaining human being I have ever known.

When Evan (who was six foot, seven inches tall and as big around the waist as a football player's thigh) was in his late seventies, we found ourselves in the midst of the largest inhabited area in the world into which only a handful of civilized human beings has ever set foot.

A half-dozen staff members of The Institutes from Philadelphia, my chosen brother Dr. Raymundo Veras (who was the Medical Director of The Institutes in Brazil), along with those superb pioneers and explorers, the Villas Boas brothers, had been dropped at the Xingu River base camp by the Brazilian Air Force, who dropped supplies to us along the way.

We left our base camp that morning and marched nine miles through steaming wet savannah and saw grass to find the village of a tiny tribe of Xinguanos known as the Kalapalo, to examine the children of the tribe, as we had done in hundreds of places on every continent.

The nine-mile trek to find the tribe took us through extremely high temperatures. Surrounded by swarms of hungry mosquitoes, we had to undress completely three times to cross rivers, carrying our equipment and clothing on our heads, and to re-dress while being attacked by red ants whose bites were quite painful. After hours of studying the half dozen babies and small children in the forty-member tribe of tiny but handsome Indians, we made our way back over the same nine miles and through the same three small rivers, until we at long last reached the Xingu River and our canoes to return to our base camp.

Evan Thomas was particularly attractive to mos-quitoes, and in my mind's eye I can see him as if it were happening now. He had literally hundreds of insect bites on his naked upper body and, because he was also heavily perspiring over his skinny but very tall frame, there were rivulets of red coursing down his body from the insect bites. Despite the fact that he was nearing eighty, he had insisted on carrying some of the heavy supplies and he was putting them into the canoe, chatting merrily all the while.

"Sir," I said, "you are a very uncomplaining man."

I made this comment in view of the fact that the rest of us (including me, the leader) were in spirits which ranged from touchy to murderous, due to the extreme discomforts we were experiencing. It was uncomfortable enough to make us nasty, but not uncomfortable or dangerous enough to make us cheerful and determined.

Evan Thomas unfolded himself to his full height, looked me right in the eye and pointed his long, bony index finger at me, which was a characteristic stance when he was about to deliver a message.

"On the contrary," said Evan Thomas with steel in his voice and his long index finger pointed unwaveringly at my nose, "I am a most complaining man, and as soon as I find something worth complaining about, you'll hear from me!"

He meant it.

The rest of us grinned, albeit sheepishly, as we canoed back to our base camp.

The parents of The Evan Thomas Institute are a good deal like Evan Thomas himself. They are a delightful bunch of people that the staff loves to be with; like Evan, they complain very little and only when there is something *worth* complaining about.

I can really only remember Evan Thomas complaining about two things in his life. The first was what great damned fools we human beings are capable of being when we really put our minds to it, and the second was how little time there was to do all the things which one wanted to do in one's life.

Dr. Thomas worked every day of the week, and a sixteen-hour day was more usual than it was unusual. On more than one occasion, when he was in his eighties, I would finish work at 2 A.M. and see that the light was on in his office. I would find him hunched over his desk, writing an article or a book. He'd look up, pleased to see me, and smile a welcome, too well mannered to hope that I wouldn't visit too long, so he could get back to the job at hand.

There was never enough *time* for Evan.

The Evan Thomas Institute's name doesn't so much honor Evan Thomas as Evan Thomas honors the staff of that Institute. The splendid children who are a product of that Institute are the real honor to Evan Thomas.

The parents of The Evan Thomas Institute share, to a woman and man, Evan Thomas's complaint about so little time.

So little time to teach babies all of the glorious, beautiful, profound, enthralling, and uplifting things there are in the world.

The reader may already have begun to feel that complaint of Dr. Thomas and the parents—so little time.

This chapter is a special gift from the staff to

parents, kids, and the readers. It's a gift of time which boggles the mind.

Can we really provide a baby with millions of brain connections in thirty seconds?

Indeed we can.

What can we actually do with a tiny kid and thirty seconds?

By giving him ten *related* facts, we can give him 3,628,800 connections in his knowledge bank.

How is that possible?

Well, it's due to a mathematical law called the law of combinations and permutations.

I didn't learn about it until I grew up, and perhaps you didn't either.

If that's so, let's review it briefly, because understanding it is vital to appreciating the astonishing things you can do with your baby in thirty seconds.

If I have five cards, each of a different color, I am able to set them up in a surprising number of different combinations. I can put the red one with the blue one, the red one with the yellow one, the red one with the green one, the green one with the yellow card, the green card with the blue one and so on.

The math people have a formula for this. It is 5 × 4 × 3 × 2 × 1 which amounts to 120 ways to combine the five cards.

Now if I make it six cards, the number becomes more than surprising, since there are 720 ways to combine six objects.

The number of ways I can combine seven (and now I'm forced to my annoyingly capable little calculator) is astonishing—5,040.

Eight is 40,320.

Nine is mind boggling—362,880.

Ten is 3,628,800.

Eleven is 39,916,800.

And twelve stumps even my little calculator, which doesn't go that high.

The basis of all intelligence is facts.

Without facts there can be no intelligence.

The greatest computers which exist have an intelligence estimated by the computer people to be about that of an insect called the earwig (Order: Dermaptera.)

Now let's consider that incredible computer, the human brain, which weighs three-and-a-half pounds *and has a capacity ten times greater than that of the United States national archives.*

The computer works on the exact same basis as the human brain and was, of course, modeled on the human brain. Up to now the computers are startling but remain a very poor copy of the human brain.

The human brain is the most superb of all computers and obeys the same rules. With a small number of facts it can come to a small number of conclusions. With a huge number of facts it can come to a huge number of conclusions.

If they are *related* facts the number of conclusions is breathtaking.

What things can we do with thirty seconds?

What can we *not* do with thirty seconds!

Now you mothers with little time to spend with your children, pay attention as never before.

Your little child looks out the window and sees a collie. "What's that?" he asks you.

1. We can say, "Look, baby, Mommy has to get dinner."
   It will take at least thirty seconds to get rid of the baby and make that stick.

2. We can look out the window and say, "That's a bow-wow."

   It will take at least thirty seconds to make *that one stick.*

3. We can use thirty seconds to say, "That's a dog."

   It will take at least thirty seconds to make *that one stick. At least it's true* to say, "That's a dog." However, it is far from meeting the standards. The word "dog" is *not* precise, it is *not* discrete, and it is *highly* ambiguous. If one says the word "dog" to a hundred different people, a hundred different images will appear in the mind ranging from tiny brown smooth ones to huge black and white hairy ones.

4. We can say, "That's a dog called a collie." We can then go on to tell him thirty seconds' worth of information which *is* precise, discrete, unambiguous, and true.

Number four is a fine answer and meets the requirements.

How sad it is that we put information into a computer with great skill and great precision and put information into our children's brains in a hit-or-miss, slip-shod, sloppy, and often untruthful way.

Remember also that, unlike the computer, we can never totally erase the facts which we put into our baby's brain. They will remain as the first response available on recall. They will remain if they are true and they will remain if they are untrue.

In ten seconds a skilled mother can show her child, who is familiar with the way it is done, ten different pictures. The *faster* Mother does it the *better* the child will learn.

> "Barn Swallow"
> "Collie"
> "Blood Python"
> "Sapphire"
> "George VI"
> "Borneo"
> "Michelangelo"
> "Ralph Waldo Emerson"
> "New Zealand Flag"
> "Harp"

Ten seconds—ten facts.

If mother does them on three consecutive days using one second per card, the child will be well on his way to having ten superbly clear facts stored in permanent storage.

So—in thirty seconds we can give him ten wonderful facts in contrast to saying "Get lost" or "Bow-wow."

Is that the end of it? It is hardly the beginning.

To tell you the glorious truth and to make it understandable we must make a supposition which is actually improbable but in no way invalidates the point we should like to make. Suppose your child were a perfectly normal two-year-old who had never seen a dog in his life.

Now you are going to have one of the ten seconds teaching sessions you both love.

You have prepared ten cards each of which contains a clear and first-rate picture of a breed of dogs.

These ten Bits of Intelligence are different from the previous ten in that they are all dogs. In short, they are ten *related* facts. They are like ten cards of different colors.

Here you go with your ten seconds and ten pictures of different kinds of dogs.

"Bobby, these are all pictures of dogs."

"Dachshund"
"St. Bernard"
"Labrador Retriever"

"Schnauzer"
"Cocker Spaniel"
"German Shepherd"
"Boxer"
"Doberman Pinscher"
"Samoyed"
"Pekinese"

Ten seconds—three consecutive days, thirty seconds.

Now you go out on the street together with Bobby who has never actually seen a dog and down the street comes a Chesapeake Bay Retriever. Does anybody doubt for a moment that Bobby will point excitedly and say, "Mommy, Mommy, a DOG."

Don't doubt it. He will.

He will not of course say, "Chesapeake Bay Retriever."

He has never seen or heard of that kind of dog. But he *has* heard of and seen dogs. He has learned them superbly. But how it is possible for him to recognize this dog, even as a dog?

You have taught him ten dogs. He knows all the things that dogs have in common. Four legs, heads, tails, hair, etc. He also knows that dogs come in many colors, with big ears, little ears, short tails, long tails, hairy, shaggy, smooth, and so on.

You have given him ten dogs which he has now combined and permutated. He has exactly *three million, six hundred and twenty-eight thousand, eight hundred ways of combining and permutating them.*

Are you thunder-struck?

If you're *not,* then we've presented the case poorly indeed.

Has he got *room* for all of that?

He has.

He has a brain capacity of one hundred and twenty-five trillion facts (125,000,000,000,000).

Parents who find themselves either puzzled or fascinated by this and who, as a result of being either fascinated or mystified wish to learn about the brain's capacity and about the use of facts and neural connections actually to grow the brain should read *How to* Multiply *Your Baby's Intelligence* (New York: Doubleday, 1984.)

Remember also that his brain grows by precisely this kind of use.

Are you saying, "But surely he'll never use the whole 3,628,800 of them."

Perhaps not. If you'd tell us how many and which ones he *is* going to use, perhaps we can find a way to teach him just those. But why should we limit him?

Ever buy a dictionary or an encyclopedia? How many words or facts have you ever actually looked up? A thousand? Why didn't you just buy a book that only had the thousand you were going to use? Were you ever out of your house where you kept the dictionary or encyclopedia and wished you had it?

How would you like to have an encyclopedia in your *head,* especially knowing that the brain *grows* by use?

Is having a huge number of facts, then, all there is to it? Of course not. We all have met somebody in our lives who has a head full of facts and doesn't have enough sense to come in out of the rain.

But that doesn't alter the fact that the degree of intelligence we have will be limited to the things which can be determined from the number of facts we have.

Let's summarize what you can do with thirty seconds.

1. Tell him to get lost.
2. Tell him it's a bow-wow.

3. Tell him it's a dog.
4. Tell him it's a collie.
5. Teach him ten superb facts.
6. Teach him ten *related* facts.

Thus giving him 3,628,800 ways to combine and permutate those ten facts and growing his brain every time he does.

Do we hear you sighing with relief—and perhaps smiling with anticipation—knowing what you can do with thirty seconds?

Have fun—it's vital to success.

12

motivation is a product of success*

by Glenn Doman

*This chapter alone is *not* taken from the "How to Multiply Your Baby's Intelligence" lectures but instead is taken from the "What to Do About Your Brain-Injured Child" lectures which have been given to the parents of hurt children at The Institutes for more than a quarter of a century.

motivation is a product
of success

It took me a long time to understand it, when you consider the fact that I was watching it being done so superbly all day, every day, of my life. As a matter of fact, I was doing it pretty well myself, without being able to explain it to myself.

It took me until 1955 to understand what I was seeing because the world was telling me one thing while I was living with its opposite.

The world was telling me that:

"Success is a product of motivation. Highly motivated people succeed because they are motivated. Poorly motivated people fail because they are poorly motivated."

What I was seeing, hearing, and feeling every moment of my life was that the opposite was true. What I was watching daily was that:

High motivation is a product of success.
Low motivation is a product of failure.

The only mothers I was seeing in those days were my incredibly motivated mothers of the brain-injured children.

The obvious reason why *they* were motivated to do near-miracles was clear to me. They were so highly motivated because they had brain-injured children and had been told everywhere they had been in the world that their children were hopeless.

They hadn't believed that, and had searched the state, country, continent, or world until they had found us.

We had told them it was not necessarily hopeless,

had designed programs for them, and had sent them home to do them.

Their children were successful in moving, speaking, understanding, breathing, seeing, hearing, and thinking and they were delighted.

One of the things that surprised me back in those days was that very few of those mothers ever asked me about how to motivate their babies, considering how much everybody else talks about it.

I suppose the reason why my particular mothers rarely asked me about motivation was that they were already experienced; being the mothers of brain-injured children who were sometimes so severely injured that they had to be encouraged to breathe, my mothers were among the world's leading experts on motivating children.

Not being a mother of a brain-injured child, nor even a female, I was not equipped by nature to understand motivation instinctively, nor were the professionals who were my teachers able to enlighten me. I learned about motivation by experience, observation, and thought. Not being able to handle it by instinct, it was necessary for me to define it in words. It is frequently advantageous to be able to put words to instinctive reactions. I am now able to talk about motivation and dare to do so to some of the best motivating mothers in the whole world. Frequently, the mothers who are the best instinctive motivators are the most grateful for being able to evaluate their own actions in words.

When on occasion one of my mothers does raise the question of motivation, she almost invariably puts the question properly: "How," she asks, "can I motivate my child?" The very way she puts the question indicates that she knows the most important part of the answer. She does not ask why her child wasn't born motivated. Her question makes it clear that she believes that the problem of motivation lies within herself rather than being inborn with the child. She already knows the big secret.

She *knows* the truth.

The world believes that motivation is familial and inbred. It's a convenient thought. It's an easy thought. It would explain a lot. The only problem for me is that I don't believe it. I've lived in too many huts in too many jungles and too many deserts to believe it. It conflicts with all I see. It conflicts with all I know. It conflicts, I think, with the facts.

It is *not* that motivation begets success and that lack of motivation begets failure. It is quite the other way round. Success *creates* motivation. Failure *destroys* motivation.

I have watched the fascinating process by which the brain-injured child pounds his way to function as a salmon beats his way up impossible waterfalls against enormous odds. For more than a quarter century I have been a privileged observer of the brain-injured child trying to crawl across a room on his belly, moving against paralysis, against uncontrollable and unwanted movements, with incomplete vision, incomplete hearing, incomplete sensation, using his fingernails, his toenails, his teeth, using even the uncontrolled and unwanted movement if this chaotic flopping happens to push him forward and struggling onward against it when it pushes him backward.

Although I have watched this Olympian struggle on the part of a tiny child thousands of times, I remain forever involved as I sit silently watching. My knuckles whiten, my nails dig deep into my palms, I bite my lip, I am drenched in perspiration, I strain forward in my chair trying to push this heroic little child forward by my will if not by my prayer. Ten minutes pass and the struggle to crawl twenty feet continues and the tension increases as the child, against overwhelming odds, approaches the wall which is his goal. In my heart I cheer for him. I am not religious, but I pray for him. By God, I ask myself, why does he continue to try to gain so little at such cost in superhuman effort? But, by

God, how I do admire this endlessly determined little bundle of terribly hurt humanity.

His hand flies out and touches the wall and the room explodes in wild applause. My office is filled with joy; parents, graduate students, physicians, staff are on their feet applauding, laughing, congratulating, and I find my own eyes wet with emotion for this little child. Not for a moment do I feel pity, which is a cheap and plentiful emotion; it is admiration which moves me to tears and, more than that, it is respect which courses down my cheek. No ballerina, no concert pianist, no Shakespearean actor in all of history ever received a more spontaneous or sincere ovation than this little bundle of hurt humanity now receives—and deserves.

I have, as I have said, experienced this drama thousands of times, and today I feel it not less but more than the first time I beheld this miracle of sorts, more than a quarter century ago. I suppose I *appreciate* it more.

I have been privileged to behold miracles of motivations, and I have watched those superb motivators, the mothers, countless times. And I have learned much.

I have learned that such monumental motivation has simple enough beginnings, simple not only in the children but in me, for in many ways I am childlike.

Strange fellow that I am (as compared with you), I find myself with an extremely clear-cut view about success and failure. I find myself carefully avoiding doing those things at which I fail and repeating over and over again those things which I do well.

I *know* I should not. I *know* I should work hard at those things at which I fail so as to accomplish them and avoid spending time at those things at which I invariably succeed since I am already accomplished at them. I *know* I would be a better person and that I would become more rounded if I did it the other way around.

Still, it occurs to me that I am round enough, and so I continue to avoid those things at which I fail and to return again and again to those things at which I succeed. I am sure that you do not behave in such an *undetermined* way. But I do.

I have never learned to play tennis nor can I carry a tune, and, despite all the insistence of my friends who play tennis beautifully or who sing superbly that I could easily learn, no one in the last forty years has succeeded in getting me onto a tennis court or to sing publicly since Miss Jeffries, my first grade teacher, blew her pitch pipe to give us "do" and then looked pained—and in my direction. I know I could learn if I wanted to. I just don't want to. I note with interest that all my friends who want to get me onto a tennis court play tennis beautifully and those who would head me for the concert stage sing beautifully.

I continue to avoid the things at which I fail. It's a weakness which I intend to keep.

On the other hand there are some things I do well and a few things that I do extremely well, and I know it. Try as I may to avoid it, I find myself doing those things over and over and over again. It goes like this. I do whatever it is that I do well. Since I *know* I do it well, I do it completely and confidently. It is almost always a pleasure to see something done well, and so when I am done you say, "Golly, but you did that well."

"Yes, I did do that rather well, didn't I?" I say. "Would you like to see me do that again?"

And so it goes.

In my weakness I am just like the kids whether they are overtly brain-injured or whether they are not. They also tend to avoid that at which they fail while repeating over and over again that at which they succeed.

By the very nature of the severely brain-injured child's brain injury, he is a born loser. He can frequently do absolutely nothing except breathe, and he almost always does that rather badly. Failure is the story of his life until help comes.

Now let us suppose that for some reason it would be a good idea to have a little brain-injured girl wrap her hands around a ¾ ″ bar and hang, feet down, supporting her weight from her hands. (This is, in fact, a first-rate idea for all children of all sizes and shapes and is a highly sophisticated idea which the staff of The Institutes for the Achievement of Human Potential in Philadelphia spent many years developing.) Suppose, in fact, that your child, a four-year-old, let's say, is a patient at The Institutes in Philadelphia and that we have instructed you on the importance of her learning to hang by her hands for one minute even though she is unable to move and unable to speak.

Being a first-rate set of parents, you are most anxious to give your tiny paralyzed daughter every opportunity to be a whole functioning human being. Indeed, you would give anything in the world to bring that about.

Now you build a bar in a doorway a few inches higher than her total height with arms outstretched. You say a little prayer, "Please Lord, let her win just this once!" You are ready to begin.

"Now, honey, I am going to put your hands around this bar and you must hold on for one minute the way all your friends in Philadelphia want you to do. Once you get a grip, I'll let go of you, and it will be just as if you are standing up all by yourself for the first time in your life only your feet won't be touching the floor. Don't worry, honey, because when you can't hold on any longer, I'll catch you, so you don't have to worry. Here we go, honey!"

With your heart in your mouth and a prayer on your lips, you, Mother, open her little hands while your husband supports her weight and you wrap them around the bar.

Now you let go and Mary hangs for exactly one-half second before falling into her father's outstretched arms.

"Oh, no, honey," you protest, "that was only one-half a second, and you've got to hang one whole minute. It's so important." To her father you say, "What are we going to *do*? She *must* hang more than a hundred times that long. How will we ever motivate her to do it?"

Now let's look at that perfectly natural episode from Mary's standpoint. Mary is four years old. Being severely brain-injured, she is very small, as brain-injured children are inclined to be, so she weighs only twenty-six pounds. She has never crawled, crept, hung, stood, or walked in her life. She has just tried to hang for the first time in her life and succeeded for only half a second.

"Well," says tiny Mary to herself (being unable to talk), "that's failure six-thousand-four-hundred and ninety-two. I failed again! That's the story of my life."

Mary, being very hurt, may not be able to articulate it quite that clearly, but that is precisely what she'll feel. What else could she *possibly* think under that set of circumstances?

What we have *told* her is the amount by which she is less than perfect. She has missed perfection by fifty-nine-and-one-half seconds.

We have told her by how much she *failed.*

Now suppose we ask ourselves a question. Just how long *should* a paralyzed, speechless, brain-injured four-year-old child with the body of a two-year-old be able to hang from a bar the first time she tries it? How long should *any* little four-year-old hang, for that matter?

Well, it is obvious that you don't know and neither do I. If we don't know how long she should be able to hang, it is pretty obvious that *she* doesn't. While I don't know that answer in advance for any one little girl, I know without question that for some little girls the first time out, one-half second is a very long time to hang.

Now let's suppose that instead of the "Gosh,

honey, that just isn't good enough" approach, you—her mother—had used a different approach.

Suppose at the end of that one-half second when Mary dropped into Dad's arms, you had taken her into your arms and said, "Wow!"

Suppose you had hugged her and kissed her and said, "Who would have *dreamed* that a tiny little girl like *you* could have hung on to that bar for a whole half second?"

Suppose you had told her she was a most extraordinary little girl. Suppose you had told her that she was without question the most remarkable child in the whole city, probably the most magnificent child in the entire state, and possibly the best little girl in the whole *world.*

Suppose you had told her with love and with respect.

Suppose also that you *meant* it. Do you know any other little four-year-old girl who can't move and can't talk who ever even *tried* to hang by her hands?

Suppose, in short, you had told her how much she had *succeeded* by.

Let's not play games with whether a speechless four-year-old girl understands what it means to be the most remarkable child in all the city. *She'll* understand the real message. When you squeeze her to your breast you'll feel nice and warm and soft and she'll get the message. When she sees the love and respect on your face for her superb accomplishment, she'll get that message. When she hears the love and respect in your voice, she'll get that message, and she doesn't need to understand a word of English to do so.

We adults make the mistake of listening to each other's words to some degree, and we are thus misled when some other adult chooses to mislead us. But nobody really fools kids because when they are listening for important messages (rather than mere information), they don't really listen to the words. They listen to the music.

Considering the two possible approaches, it's immediately obvious that in *either* case she hung for one-half second. We have no way of knowing whether that's good or bad, really, but we do know this. You may look at what she did from two very different vantage points.

If, in your anxiety to get it right for her own good, you insist on looking at the difference between the way she *is* the first time she tries this new and important treatment and the way you *want* her to be, then you can only bemoan the fact that it is not good enough.

If such is the case, then you must not be surprised when Mary says to herself, "Yep, that's my six-thousand-four-hundred and ninety-second failure, and now the big ones are going to keep at me with this new damned business at which I will now fail as many times a day as they make me do it. It's the story of my life."

And she will.

That's what *I* do.

Now if, on the other hand, what you want is for her to do it again and again and to attack it with enthusiasm and to want to do it again and again, then you might be wise to look at it from the vantage point of where she was yesterday and where she *is* today.

Yesterday nobody would have dreamed of asking this immobile and speechless little girl to hang by her hands at all. Today she can support her own weight by hanging from her hands for a full half second. When *you* appreciate the miracle that has happened and show your respect for that accomplishment, then surely Mary will glow with the pleasure of accomplishment and of Mommy's praise and then she will say with or without words:

"Yes, I did do that well, didn't I? Would you like to see me do it again?"

And she will.

That's what *I* do.

It is you, Mother, who *decides* what success or failure is.

If you want to win in raising your child to be superb then look at the difference between where she is and where you want her to be, *don't* pound the child's ear about that. That is *your* problem and *mine*. Pointing out how far the child has yet to go makes it sound as if how *far* to go were her fault.

Thus, we have the formula: failure which leads to losing which leads to lack of motivation which leads to her stubbornly refusing to try. Or, as Mary puts it, "That's the story of my life."

If, on the other hand you want to motivate Mary to try and try and try again until she can hang on a bar for a minute or walk or talk or read or write, then it behooves you to look at where she is today versus where she was before you started such an intensive program, which is to say the difference between the way she *is* and the way she *was,* and you must be grateful and enthusiastic and respectful and joyous.

Thus we have the formula: success which leads to winning which leads to motivation which leads to her actually wanting to do it again and looking forward to doing it again. Or, as Mary puts it, "Yes, I did do that well, didn't I? Would you like to see me do it again?"

If you would like to see her do whatever it is again, try rewarding her with your love and praise.

That is what she wants, and what *every* kid wants, more than anything else in the world.

So it was that we learned about motivation being the result, rather than the cause, of success.

For ten long years I had thought how lucky we were that we always seemed to get such highly motivated kids (such as the little boy crawling across the room for the first time against such overwhelming odds) with such highly motivated parents, and how lucky we were to have such a highly motivated staff willing to work such dreadfully long hours and to work so hard.

It took me a long time (ten years) to realize that getting such highly motivated staff, parents, and kids had nothing to do with luck. It had to do with success.

Because the kids were now doing things which they had never before in their lives been able to do, the parents were overjoyed.

Because the parents were overjoyed they told the kids how marvelous and successful they were.

Because the kids succeeded, they became highly motivated.

Because the parents were succeeding in doing things with their children which had never been achieved before in history, the staff was overjoyed.

Because the staff was overjoyed, they told the parents how marvelous and successful they were.

Because the parents succeeded, they became highly motivated.

Because the staff was successfully teaching parents how to do things which no group in history had ever taught them before, the parents were overjoyed.

Because the parents were overjoyed, they told the staff how marvelous and successful they were.

Because the staff succeeded, they became highly motivated.

If you want your kid to be highly motivated, all you do is arrange for him always to win.

You do this by telling him how much he has succeeded by (how far he has moved *towards* perfection, rather than how far he still has to go).

It won't be necessary for you to tell him how much he failed by, or how big a loser he is. The school system will take care of that for you. They will spend *twelve years* telling him how much he fails by. "No, stupid, that is *not* the way you spell Mediterranean."

What *you* want to do is to make him so highly motivated by the time he gets to school, by arranging for him to *win* all the time, that not even the school system can knock it out of him thereafter by arranging for him to *lose* all the time.

But of course, being a parent, you always knew all of that in your heart, and I'm sure you've almost always practiced it, but I just thought I ought to mention it.

How do you do that for a well baby in a practical and day-by-day way?

Try what the next chapter says.

13

how to motivate your baby

by Janet Doman
Susan Aisen

how to motivate your baby

There are three major areas concerned with the intellectual as compared with the physical side of human intelligence.

The first is reading and of all things reading is the most important. Reading is the very *basis* of all those things which are considered *the liberal arts,* as well as the area of human ability which the school system is most likely to fail.

The second is general knowledge and all human intelligence is based upon the facts which *constitute* human knowledge. Without facts *there can be no intelligence.*

The third is mathematics and is the basis for all science.

This chapter deals with the general rules for teaching *all three* of these things.

It deals with how you should *deal* with your child and how you should *feel* about your child. It also deals with how you should feel about yourself.

The better you feel about your child and yourself and the better you understand what this chapter *says* and *means,* the greater will be your success.

We are so much a product of our own education that sometimes in teaching our children we unwittingly make the same mistakes that were the cause of so much suffering for us.

The school system arranges for kids to fail. We can all remember the big red "X's" on all the wrong answers. Correct answers often received no mention at all. Tests were given with the intention of exposing our ignorance rather than discovering our knowledge.

In order to enjoy thoroughly the unalloyed thrill

of teaching your tiny child it is best to begin with a clean slate. Here is a guide for your success:

1. *Teach him because you think it's a great idea and a privilege for you.*

If this idea appeals to you then go ahead and plunge in. Take your phone off the hook and put a sign on your front door that reads "Silence— Professional Mother at Work—Do Not Disturb." If you want to become a professional mother you will be joining the oldest and most venerable profession in the world. If you believe it's a privilege to teach your child, you should avail yourself of that privilege.

If you don't like this idea—if there is anything about it that feels like a *duty*—don't do it. It won't work. You won't like it. Your kid won't like it. It isn't for everyone.

2. *Talk clearly, loudly, and with great enthusiasm.*

Since you've decided that teaching your child is your idea of fun, make sure it always shows. Don't be subtle with your tiny child. Use a nice, clear, loud voice infused with all the enthusiasm that you actually feel. It should be easy for your child to hear you and to appreciate your enthusiasm.

If you have a quiet, unenthusiastic voice—change it. Create enthusiasm in your voice and your child will absorb it from you like a sponge.

3. *Relax and enjoy yourself.*

This is the greatest game there is. The fact that it results in vast and important changes in your tiny child should not make it "serious" for you. You and your child have nothing to lose and everything to gain.

As your child's teacher you should make sure you eat and sleep enough to be relaxed and enjoy yourself. Being tense is usually a result of fatigue, disorganization, or not having a good enough understanding of *why* you are doing what you are doing.

All these things are easily remedied and should be if you are not enjoying yourself. In this regard for your child's sake you may have to become a bit more conscious of your own well-being than you might have been previously.

4. *Trust your kid—show it in your attitude, manner, and actions.*

Your kid trusts you, often completely and absolutely. Return that trust. He wants to learn more than anything in the world even when it may appear that he wishes to drive you crazy. When you trust your child's eagerness to learn and his tremendous ability, your attitude, manner, and actions will reflect this.

If you doubt your child's abilities you should not be doing this program in the first place.

5. *Constantly give him new information.*

Perhaps this is the single most overlooked ingredient of success. New information is the spice of every program. When new information is plentiful, you and your child will be flying along. There will never be enough hours in a day or days in a week. Your child's world will be in a constant state of expansion. This is what every child is aiming for, every day of his life.

6. *When he knows old information, put it away.*

If you cannot provide new information because you are moving or having a new baby or whatever, don't keep pushing the old things. Put them away. When you have something new, then and only then, begin again.

7. *Teach him with purpose and in a highly organized way.*

Your enjoyment will be largely related to your level of organization. A highly organized mother has a strong sense of purpose about what she is doing. She knows exactly what she has done, how many times she has done it, and when it is time to move on. She has a good supply of new information ready and waiting whenever she needs it.

Very fine professional mothers sometimes fall by the wayside only because they never take the time to sit down and get themselves organized. What a tragedy this is because if they did organize themselves they would discover they are fine teachers who are being held back only by minor organizational problems.

8. *Make materials large and easy to see.*

Your materials should always reflect the state of your child's visual development at that moment. Wise mothers always make their materials larger and easier to see than may be strictly necessary, just to be safe.

Materials that are of poor quality, unclear, or so

small that they are difficult to see will not be learned easily. This will decrease the pleasure of teaching and learning.

9. *Provide an environment free from visual, auditory, and tactile distractions.*

Most households are not quiet places. However it is possible to decrease the level of chaos in a household. You should turn off the television, radio, and record-player while you are teaching. Make an area free from visual chaos that is your major teaching area.

Be ready to go when you start a session so you aren't your own worst distraction.

The world sometimes confuses stimulation with chaos. Stimulation is excellent for your baby— chaos is not.

10. *Teach him only at the times when he is happy and well.*

You know your child better than anyone else on the face of the earth. You know when he is full of zest and you know when he is a little bit off. Always choose the very best moments to teach him.

Never teach him when you see he is a little off. In tiny babies teething is often a time of pain and sleeplessness. Never teach your child during a particular time of pain. It is a real mistake to think you can teach anything to a human being who is sick, poorly rested, or in pain.

Sometimes mother and child are enjoying their program so much that *both* try to persist through such periods. Do not attempt this.

There are so many good times and they so heavily outweigh the few bad times that you should use the best only and avoid the rest.

11. *Always show the materials very, very quickly.*

We all underestimate the lightning speed of tiny kids. Practice makes perfect and the more you teach your child the faster he will be able to go. It is absolutely vital to your success that you zoom through your materials. Speed and enjoyment are inextricably linked in the learning process. Anything that speeds this process will raise the enjoyment.

Conversely anything that slows it down will *decrease* enjoyment. A slow session is a deadly session. It is an insult to the learning ability of a tiny child and will be interpreted as such by him.

Mother and father should practice on each other before beginning with their little one. This will insure great speed right at the start.

12. *Always stop before he wants to stop.*

As mentioned earlier, this is a *major point* in success. Only you can control the amount of materials and the length of the session. Do yourself and your child a huge favor and always fall short of the number of items he would like in a session. He should always consider that you are a little bit stingy with information. There is never enough, consequently he *always* wants more. This is the correct set of dynamics for your program. Anything less than this is not acceptable.

All tiny kids would, if permitted, glut themselves. This is why you will get cries of "More!" and "Again!" This is a sign of success. You will maintain your success by *not* giving in to these demands (at least not *immediately*). Promise to come back in five minutes. Ask him to complete something that needs doing first, then you can do the Bits again.

The tyranny of a tiny child can enter in here. When it does, remember you are the mother of the household and as such the purveyor of Bits and reading words, et cetera. Don't allow your child to set up the dynamics of the program. That is your responsibility. He will not decide wisely—you will. He is the best learner there is—*you* are the best teacher.

13. *Trust he knows the things you have taught him.*

If you have followed your program properly, you should garnish your hard work and success with the absolute trust that your kid has taken in what you have given him. This is really not a huge step to take. It is rather like saying, "Recognize that he can see the nose on his face." Of course he knows what you've told him and shown him. You have gone to some considerable effort to make it all nice and clear, precise, discrete, and unambiguous. What else could he do but know it? It is all so simple for him. How nice it is for him to see that *you* know this is so!

14. *Be on his side—bet on him.*

When in doubt, bet on your kid. You will always be a winner and, even more important, so will he. The whole world is betting against the little kid; betting he doesn't understand, betting he doesn't remember, betting he doesn't "get it." Your child doesn't need one more person on *that* team!

15. *Always be willing to change your approach. Make each day new and exciting.*

A tiny child changes every single day. As information comes in at a tremendous rate he uses that information to put two and two together. This process is taking place *all* day *every* day. Sometimes we get a glimpse of him doing something he has never done before or an insight into some new way he has of looking at the world. Whether we are lucky enough to see it or not his abilities literally *multiply* daily. Just as you are becoming comfortable with one way of doing something he is getting it all figured out and naturally wants something fresh. You and I like to find a nice cozy rut and stay in it for a while. Tiny kids *always* want to move ahead.

So when you have a nice routine that you like you will probably have to toss all the cards up in the air and revamp for the new kid who woke up this morning.

Probably when you say "Good night" to your kid each evening you *should* say "Good-bye." He won't be the same tomorrow. Make sure you have a new routine to go with your new kid.

16. *Present knowledge as a privilege that he has earned.*

The things you are teaching your child are precious. Knowledge is not valuable—it is *invaluable*. Once a mother asked us, "Should I always give my child a kiss after I've taught him something?"

Our reply was, "Kiss him as often as you like. Actually your question is a little like asking 'Should I give him a kiss after I kiss him?' "

Now you have another way of showing the most profound of all forms of affection—respect. Each time you teach your child the spirit in which you do so should be that of a kiss or a hug. Your teaching is so much a part of everything you do with your child. It begins when he wakes up and doesn't end until he is sound asleep. When he is in good form you learn together. When he is giving you a hard time, put your materials away until you and he have come to a meeting of minds.

17. *Always, always, always tell him the truth.*

Your child was born thinking everything you say is true. Never give him any reason to revise his thinking on this subject.

Don't allow anyone else to give him anything less than the truth either. The reason for this should be obvious.

18. *Always keep a promise that you make.*

Since you have infinite respect for your child it is only right that your child should return that respect. If you keep your word in all things, all the time, he will respect you. If you do not, he may love you but he will not respect you. What a shame to deprive him of that joy.

19. *Give him the correct answer rather than jumping on the wrong one.*

From time to time your child may come to an incorrect conclusion or a wrong answer. When this happens, gently give him the correct answer without any great commotion.

Don't say, "No, that isn't the Australian flag."

Instead say, "This is the New Zealand flag, isn't it?"

If he did not know the correct answer, you have just supplied it. He will be happy to have that missing information.

20. *Don't test him.*

If your child wants to show you what he knows and you *both* enjoy designing games with your materials then you can proceed to do so, but with *caution.*

When he volunteers an answer, of course your enthusiasm should be obvious. You should be saying to yourself, "Wow. If he knew that there are fifty other things just like that which he must know."

If he begins to give incorrect answers, particularly where he has succeeded easily in the past, you should harbor a deep suspicion that he is pulling your leg. *This usually only occurs when you keep playing the same game over and over again. It means he is bored.*

If, in order to spice up the game, he starts to reverse the rules and give wrong answers, a smart mother will either stop at once or if he really is enjoying himself, she will say, "You keep all the wrong answers and I'll have the correct ones!" Now you are both on the same team again where you belong.

If you actually do fall into the trap of testing your child, you will find it is a deep abyss. Tiny children can be endlessly devious if they believe their knowledge or ability is being questioned. Testers beware! Tiny children always have the last laugh. If worst comes to worst, they will simply walk away and this is the unkindest cut of all.

21. *When he asks you a question, answer honestly, factually, and with enthusiasm.*

Your child will quickly come to the conclusion that you have all the answers. He will see you as a source of information. He is right. You are the source of information for him. When he trusts you with one of his endless, brilliant, and usually quite difficult-to-answer questions, rise to the occasion. If you know the answer—give it to him on the spot. Don't put him off if you can possibly avoid it. If you do not know the answer, tell him you don't know it. Then take the time to find the answer.

If you can't find the answer, tell him when you will find it and follow through with giving it to him.

He will quickly understand when you are giving him hard facts and when you are expressing your own viewpoint as long as you differentiate between the two. You should not be hesitant about expressing your own views—you are his mother and while he expects you to give him the facts he will also need and want your opinion as well.

It is worth remembering that you are not simply teaching your child all that is worth knowing in this world, you are also teaching your grandchildren's father how to teach them. It is a humbling thought.

14

the importance of bits
of intelligence

by Glenn Doman

the importance of bits
of intelligence

In order for a Bit of Intelligence to *be* a true Bit of Intelligence it must be—

1. Precise.
2. Discrete.
3. Unambiguous.
4. Splendidly done.

When such is the case, it becomes a precious addition to your child's encyclopedic knowledge and a rock-firm building block in your child's brain growth and life-long education upon which thousands of future blocks will be built.

A positive and certain way to make all staff members wince is for someone to refer to a splendidly conceived and constructed Bit of Intelligence as a "flash card."

The staff's reaction would be very similar to that which would occur if one were talking to a Shakespearian scholar and compared a paragraph of poorly written instructions on a paint can to a paragraph of Henry V's speech prior to the Battle of Agincourt. People do occasionally compare a true Bit of Intelligence to a "flash card." This occurs because you present a Bit of Intelligence in less than a full second. So do you with flash cards. The similarity ends there, just as the paragraph on the paint can is similar to the paragraph of Shakespeare only in that they are both paragraphs.

A superbly prepared Bit of Intelligence, such as a faithful reproduction of *The Last Supper,* deserves to be properly preserved and treated with great respect by both parent and child. It is neither to be "played with" nor is it to be chewed upon, any more than a fine dictionary is to be "played with" or chewed upon.

The parent's respect for both the child and for splendid knowledge can begin to be transmitted to the child by the visible respect the parent uses in dealing with the child and with the Bits of Intelligence as she or he deals with the child.

It will speak louder than words to the baby.

Indeed when the staff began, during the early 1960s, to create Bits of Intelligence which were initially in the form of written words, their respect for them as the primary and most important means of teaching tiny children rose and rose.

Long conversations took place among the staff members which centered on the importance of Bits as new Categories arose and multiplied. Since hundreds of staff hours were spent in locating suitably fine material, mounting, and labeling them, as The Institutes' library of Bits grew from hundreds to thousands and to tens of thousands, that respect grew apace.

In the end an entire department of artists and workers was created to carry out this task.

As respect for the Bits of Intelligence and the awesome job they were doing for babies and tiny children grew greater, discussions began to center on the fact that Bits of Intelligence are, to babies, what the *Encyclopaedia Britannica* is to adults. So often did this comparison arise that it seemed obvious that an alliance of some sort should actually exist between The Institutes and *Encyclopaedia Britannica*.

In the early 1960s Glenn Doman met with James Ertel, who was the editor-in-chief of *Encyclopaedia Britannica* Yearbooks, to discuss the wisdom and possibility of such a relationship.

Discussions of an unofficial nature continued until the beginning of 1980 when serious negotiations began for a contractual arrangement.

The present contractual relationship which exists between The Institutes for the Achievement of Human Potential and *Encyclopaedia Britannica* is both a natural relationship and a splendid one.

Both organizations are dedicated to the spread of knowledge and education. Where should that process more logically begin than with newborn babies?

The Institutes have spent more than forty years in gaining *unique* knowledge of how children learn from the day of birth and how that learning actually develops the child's brain.

Encyclopaedia Britannica has spent more than two hundred years codifying human knowledge and has in its possession more that twelve billion five hundred million bits of information.

All parents who wish to give their babies the greatest opportunity to develop their own knowledge and abilities to the highest levels will be delighted to learn that they will now be able to supplement their own Divisions, Categories, Sets, Bits of Intelligence, and Programs of Intelligence by purchasing splendid, already prepared materials, from The Institutes or from *Encyclopaedia Britannica.*

This will result in huge savings of time for parents. Many parents report (both joyfully and hectically) that they sometimes spend three hours a day preparing Sets of Bits of Intelligence which their children easily commit to memory in fifteen minutes.

Superbly researched and created Bits of Intelligence are the basis of the Home Library of Knowledge which should be a splendid family heritage. The next chapter tells you how to create such a library.

15

the home library of knowledge
a family heritage

by Glenn Doman

the home library of knowledge
a family heritage

The Institutes for the Achievement of Human Potential have by the terms of their own constitution as a federally tax-exempt non-profit organization, the objective of "raising the abilities of *all* children in intellectual, physical, and social terms."

By the terms of The Institutes' constitution that objective is to be accomplished in the following ways:

I   To discover *the ways in which it is possible to raise children's abilities.*

During the past forty years, The Institutes' staff has led the world in discovering hundreds of methods of raising children's abilities, often against the opposition of those who now practice the principles and methods they once so loudly opposed. The staff continues to develop new and better methods.

II   To demonstrate *the effectiveness of these methods by directly teaching parents to raise the abilities of their own children.*

The parents and children of The Evan Thomas Institute (in both the Early Development Program [On-Campus] and The International School [On-Campus]) demonstrate that this can be done. The splendidness of those children in intellectual, physical, and social terms is a totally convincing and profoundly clear demonstration that parents of ordinary background, using knowledge, love, respect and joy *can* and in fact *do* make their children intellectually superb, physically breathtaking, and socially enchanting.

Although each time I have the opportunity to watch them read in many languages, do Olympic routines on the balance beam, do math better than their parents, swim, demonstrate their incredible encyclopedic knowledge, do back flips on the mats with total control of their bodies, demonstrate the breadth and depth of their knowledge of art, do ballet so beautifully that my heartbeat increases, demonstrate their ability to solve problems which I have difficulty even understanding, play the violin individually and in concert with such soul-stirring ability, I say to myself, "I have seen this a hundred times and they could not possibly improve on the last performance. *This* time I shall not find myself moved." But I am wrong, and each time they bring tears to my eyes.

To say that, in a social sense, I am charmed by Katie, Jason, Micah, Heather, Vikki, Chip, Cara, Harry, Colleen, Marc Mihai, Donna, Alicia, Michelle, Nicholas, Michael, and all the rest would be the understatement of my life.

III   To actually teach *the parents of* all *children, from whatever nation and whether well or hurt, how to raise their children's abilities and intelligence.*

Parents and children both hurt and well come to The Institutes from all over the world and have been doing so for many decades. More than twelve thousand families have actually been seen at The Institutes for periods ranging from a single week's course, "How to Multiply Your Baby's Intelligence" presented for the parents of average children by The Better Baby Institute, to periods lasting many years of teaching the parents of hurt children (this is done in several one-week sessions per year). Obviously the number of families The Institutes are capable of seeing is extremely limited. The Institutes are limited to *actually* seeing about a thousand families a year. This limit is imposed by the necessity for the highest quality service, and by limitation of staff time, energy, and finance.

IV   *To* disseminate *the knowledge that children can be made superior to every parent alive who wishes to know it.*

It is clear that there are millions of parents in the world who would wish to make their children intellectually, physically, and socially splendid if they knew it could be done, but who could not possibly get to Philadelphia, or even to the United States, under any circumstance. By the terms of their constitution, The Institutes must and do meet this obligation.

The Institutes meet this obligation by:

A   *Writing books* on each of the subjects it has pioneered in teaching parents how to multiply their babies' abilities. As an example, *How to Teach Your Baby to Read* has been (or is presently being) published in more than twenty languages. Millions of parents have bought that book, and hundreds of thousands have actually taught their babies to read, using it as their sole knowledge. The Institutes' staff has written and continues to write books on all the discoveries made there. These books can be read by parents unable to come to Philadelphia, by getting such books from the library without charge or by buying those books inexpensively (most of them cost about US $10.00 in hardback).

B The Institutes have permitted a complete video tape course, "How to Multiply Your Baby's Intelligence," to be made, so that the entire course can be taken elsewhere in the United States and in other nations, in order that parents in Australia, Columbia, Brazil, and on the west coast of the United States may take that course and actually receive certification as Professional Parents.

C Video cassette tapes on "How to Teach Your Baby to Read," "How to Teach Your Baby Encyclopedic Knowledge," "How to Teach Your Baby Math," etc., are available and may be used as a visual supplement to the books by parents who cannot get to Philadelphia.

D Other means.

The Institutes, then, have four obligations under their constitution:

I   *To discover* new methods and principles.

II   *To demonstrate* that they work.

III   *To teach parents* directly.

IV   *To disseminate* this knowledge in such a way that it may be used by all of mankind.

We, the people of The Institutes, are persuaded that one of the most effective ways of meeting point IV (disseminating this knowledge so that every child alive may be raised in the spectrum of human neurological organization) is by the use of The Home Library of Knowledge.

In September of 1983, the Board of Directors of The Institutes for the Achievement of Human Potential directed that the staff should create and maintain in perpetuity a registry of children in order to facilitate and reinforce each individual family's ability to create and add to their individual Home Library of Knowledge.

This service, the board directed, should be available to any family in the world which requests that their child or children be registered. This registration is to be without cost to the child or family.

The Board of Directors authorized the expenditure of a maximum of $10,000. to establish that service during 1983 and 1984.

The Institutes for the Achievement of Human Potential see the establishment of home libraries of knowledge as an important step in meeting their obligations to the children of the world.

These materials, whether created by the parents themselves, The Institutes, or by *Encyclopaedia Britannica,* or by a combination of all, will constitute a home library of the highest quality which will be permanent in nature. It will be used not only by succeeding children in the same family but by succeeding generations of children.

This library for babies, tiny children, and growing children will be, to the present and future children of the world, precisely what the *Encyclopaedia Britannica* is and has been to generations of adults. It will, in fact, be the perfect introduction to the adult encyclopedia, since its basic information will be derived from the encyclopedia.

In an intellectual sense, the passing on of this library from generation to generation will be very similar to the material passing on of family silver service from generation to generation. As is the case in the traditional passing on of silver from parent to child so also will the home library grow from generation to generation just as the silver service grows from generation to generation.

THE REGISTRY

The Institutes will maintain a registry at no expense to parents which will record all acquisition of Sets, Bits, and Programs by the families and friends of each child who is registered, just as the leading jewelers of the world maintain such a registry for the patterns and pieces of silver being collected by a family.

The tremendous value to parents of such a registry seems obvious.

Parents need only make a request that their child's name be entered in The Institutes' Home Library of Knowledge Registry. They will then receive from the Registry several copies of the full list of materials available.

These lists can then be distributed to grandparents, uncles, aunts, and friends of the family with checks beside the materials which presently exist in that particular family's home library.

There are few grandparents, uncles, aunts, or

friends who have not spent many frustrating hours trying to find appropriate gifts for babies, tiny kids, and little children only to end up purchasing toys which are often not only expensive and inappropriate but which soon have parts missing, leaving parents with a problem—toys that are too expensive to discard and too bulky to store.

Using this Home Library of Knowledge Registry, grandparents and others may simply check those sets which they wish to purchase as gifts, and mail the list and accompanying order form to the Registry.

These orders will be checked against the child's registration to be sure that such a set has not been purchased by some other family member or friend.

Best of all such an organization of knowledge is one in which everyone involved wins.

The value to the child is beyond stating.

The value to the parents, as a result of the opportunity supplied to the child, is manifold.

The value of such a library to the parents will be clear to all parents who have spent hundreds of hours researching, finding, and creating Bits of Intelligence for their child. These are hours which they would much prefer to spend *using* such materials to teach their child.

Not the least of the advantages to parents is the fact that they themselves will gain a good deal of knowledge in the process of presenting such splendid information to their child.

The value to grandparents and other family members need not be pointed out to any family member who has spent time and money searching for a worthwhile gift to a child. Can one imagine a more complimentary gift to a child or to the child's parents than one which will multiply a child's intelligence?

Last of all is the value to a neighborhood, town, city, state, nation, or the world of one more superbly capable, highly knowledgeable, delightful, and humane human being.

Or tens of thousands of them.

Who can know the full value or contribution to the world of even a single such person?

SUMMARY

The purpose of this book has been to teach parents how to give their babies encyclopedic knowledge, to physically grow their brains, to multiply their intelligence, and to describe the way in which The Institutes for the Achievement of Human Potential have organized knowledge for presentation to babies, tiny kids, and little children.

This system provides a *uniform* method for that organization of knowledge so that a parent will achieve the absolute maximum of pleasure and the child the maximum of joy and learning with the *least* possible expenditure of time.

By organizing knowledge in this way the child—

1. Learns the lifetime lesson that learning is a process which is joyous beyond all other pastimes.
2. Receives a vast respect for knowledge for its own sake as well as for its ability to solve problems.
3. Builds a huge base of information on which all future learning will rest.
4. Has his knowledge built fact upon fact in an ascending and ever-widening way.
5. Gains huge knowledge in a lateral way without conscious effort of any kind as a result of the cross references between Sets from different Categories and from different Divisions.
6. Actually physically grows his or her brain as a product of the visual, auditory, and tactile stimulation he has received with frequency, intensity, and duration.

7. Has much increased intelligence as a tiny child and a huge knowledge bank on which to increase his or her intelligence for the rest of his or her life.

Examples of this are how a child learns Linnaen Classification (a binomial system of scientific nomenclature) without effort by having been presented with the phylum, class, order, family, genus, and species of each of the creatures in the Magnitudes of Information contained in the Programs of Intelligence in the Categories of Birds, Mammals, Reptiles, etc., in the Division of Biology. He learns about Carolus Linnaeus (1707–1778), the Swedish botanist who devised this system, in the Set of Great Scientists of the World from the Division of General Science. This is knowledge which most adults do *not* have upon graduation from college.

An example of how his knowledge multiplies laterally across Divisions is seen as he learns that George Washington (Set Number One—Presidents of the United States, Division—History) is from Virginia. He may already have learned about Virginia in his Set Number One—States of the United States, Division—Geography, and in Set Number One—Poisonous Reptiles of the United States, Division—Biology (the cottonmouth moccasin ranges as far north as the dismal swamp of Virginia).

The *primary* reason for the writing of this chapter is to point out to the parent who wishes to *multiply* her child's intelligence the great advantages to the child and parent of adopting a *uniform* system for organizing knowledge in a single systematic way.

No parent of limited means should feel the slightest hesitancy about launching into a full-fledged program of *multiplying* his or her child's intelligence due to a lack of funds. You are limited only by your own resourcefulness, energy, and imagination— and how you feel about your child.

At this moment there is a world, a world of great beauty, of great truth, an enchanting, beguiling, thrilling, bewitching, and enriching world of facts out there in fact land.

It is a land of great riches. There are riches for the soul, there are riches for the spirit, there are riches for science.

It is a land rich beyond imagining, but strangely it is very uncrowded. It is crowded only in spots. There are lots of artists looking at great paintings and there are lots of musicians listening to orchestras and there are lots of scientists looking at space shuttles and there are lots of doctors looking at hearts and there are lots of mathematicians looking at numbers, but very, very few people are seeing it *all.*

Only a comparatively few people are taking it *all* in.

There are a very few adults, perhaps a couple of thousand, in this rich land of facts and knowledge who with unrestrained joy and unquenchable thirst are drinking it *all* up. They're a group called "Genius." That's not so surprising—true geniuses have always been few in number and immensely curious about everything.

There are many, many more children, perhaps a hundred thousand, or perhaps several hundred thousand, in this rich land of facts and knowledge, who with unrestrained joy and unquenchable thirst are drinking it *all* up. They're the kids who, when they were babies, have had the joyous opportunity of being taught to read, to gain encyclopedic knowledge and to do math, by parents who found honest pleasure in the teaching. This group will supply the future geniuses, the highly competent adults and the future leaders of the world.

It is at once a joy and a sadness that there are a few hundred thousand of them.

It is a joy that there *are* several hundred thousand of them from whose ranks will come the truly great human beings of tomorrow, instead of the handful that there have been throughout history.

It is a sadness that there are *only* several hundred thousand of them when we realise that—

Every child born has, at the moment of birth, a higher potential intelligence than Leonardo ever used.

Every child born has a curiosity so intense that he has an absolute *rage* to learn all there is to know, and he wants to learn it right *now.*

The problem is that he wants to learn about *everything on earth* with a fine impartiality. He has a rage to learn which will never be equaled again in his life, but he has almost no taste or judgment at all. He is prepared to learn what a fly tastes like, or what Gainsborough's painting *Blue Boy* looks like. He will learn both of those things with equal ease, speed, and enthusiasm.

Your job will be to guide him to all the marvelous, true, beautiful, exciting, wise, enduring, human, and scientific things there are in that beguiling land of encyclopedic knowledge.

It is waiting for you and your child.

It is calling for you and your child.

We shall keep you from it no longer.

appendix I

Parents who wish to have their child or children entered in the Registry without charge may do so by writing to:

The Registry
c/o Robert Derr, Director
The Better Baby Institute
8801 Stenton Avenue,
Philadelphia, PA 19118 USA

Such requests should include the full name of each child to be registered, the full names of the child's parents, and the full mailing address.

Parents making such requests will receive, also without cost, as many lists of Sets of Bits of Information available at the time of registration as the parents request for distribution to families and friends.

appendix II

All of the following materials to help you teach your child may be obtained directly from The Better Baby Press by writing to:

The Better Baby Press
The Institutes for the Achievement
of Human Potential
8801 Stenton Avenue,
Philadelphia, PA 19118 USA

Books:

How to Teach Your Baby to Read
How to Give Your Baby Encyclopedic Knowledge
Teach Your Baby Math
How to Multiply Your Baby's Intelligence
What to Do About Your Brain-Injured Child

Children's Reading Books:

Good-bye Mommy
The Path to Math
Nose is Not Toes

Kits:

The Glenn Doman
How to Teach Your Baby to Read Kit

The Glenn Doman
How to Teach Your Baby Encyclopedic Knowledge Kit

The Glenn Doman
How to Teach Your Baby Math Card Set

appendix III

The Gentle Revolution *Bits of Intelligence Series*—
Available now:

Insects, Set I
Great Art Masterpieces, Set I
Great Inventors, Set I
Countries of the Americas, Set I
Musical Instruments, Set I

Available May 1984:

Birds, Set I
Art—Self-portraits, Set I
Great Inventions, Set I
Foreign Languages, Food, Set I
Organs of the Body, Set I

The seven-day "How to Multiply Your Baby's Intelligence" course, presented six times yearly on the campus of The Institutes for the Achievement of Human Potential.

Videotapes:

How to Teach Your Baby to Read
How to Give Your Baby Encyclopedic Knowledge
How to Teach Your Baby Math

Parents of brain-injured children who wish more information about the program may write to:

Douglas Doman, Vice Director
The Institutes for the Achievement
of Human Potential
8801 Stenton Avenue,
Philadelphia, PA 19118 USA

Susan Aisen   Janet Doman

Glenn Doman and Xinguano child.

about the authors

GLENN DOMAN is the founder and the present-day Chairman of Philadelphia's world-famous Institutes for the Achievement of Human Potential to which parents from every continent have been finding their way for more than a quarter of a century. It is difficult to know if he and The Institutes are more famous for their originally controversial (but now highly respected) work with brain-injured children or for their work in creating excellence in all children.

He has dealt intimately with more than twelve thousand families over the last forty years and has strongly influenced millions of families through his best-selling books which are presently published in twenty languages.

How to Teach Your Baby to Read, Teach Your Baby Math, How to Multiply *Your Baby's Intelligence,* and *What to Do About Your Brain-Injured Child* are each a classic work in the field of well children and of hurt children.

Glenn Doman has lived with, studied, or worked

with children in more than one hundred nations which have ranged from the most civilized to the most primitive. He has conducted expeditions to study pre–Stone Age children in Brazil's Mato Grosso, Bushman children in the Kalihari Desert, and Eskimo children in the Arctic, as well as journeys to see children in the world's major cities from Johannesburgh to Moscow and from London to Tokyo.

He has been decorated by many nations, often with their highest awards. It is ironic, but not inconsistent with his character, that his earliest decorations were for his role in warfare as an infantry combat officer while all of his decorations of the last thirty-five years have been for saving lives.

He was decorated by George VI with the British Military Cross for outstanding heroism in action during World War II. He received The Distinguished Service Cross from the United States for extraordinary heroism in combat, The Silver Star for gallantry against an armed enemy, and The Bronze Star for heroism in close combat. He was decorated by the Grand Duchess Charlotte for services to the Duchy of Luxembourg during the Battle of the Bulge.

In contrast to those decorations for hand-to-hand combat, he was knighted by the Brazilian government in 1966 for his services to the children of the world and received Brazil's highest decoration, The Knight Order of the Southern Cross. His services to children have also won him decorations from Britain, Ireland, Argentina, Peru, and Japan. Other honors include the Raymond A. Dart Award of the United Steelworkers of America in 1971.

He continues to maintain a staggering schedule of search for new answers, teaching, and writing.

JANET JOY DOMAN is the Director of The Institutes for the Achievement of Human Potential. She is the daughter of Glenn Doman and has been closely involved with all the programs and branches of The Institutes as they have developed and expanded.

As a teenager Janet Doman traveled and studied in Europe and South America.

She entered the University of Pennsylvania in 1967 where she majored in physical anthropology and studied under Professor Wilton Krogman for whom the Wilton Krogman Child Development Center is named. During this period she was the most junior member of The Institutes' 1969 Xingu Expedition into Brazil Centrale. She also studied zoology at the University of Hull in England before graduating from Penn in 1971.

Janet Doman then joined The Institutes' staff where she initiated The Institutes' anthropometric measurement program. Later she worked with Adelle Davis to set up the first nutritional program for The Institutes' children.

Guided by her mother, Katie Doman, Janet Doman began studies of intellectual growth and early development. In 1974 at the invitation of the Sony Corporation, Janet Doman went to Japan to teach English to tiny Japanese children. This highly successful project served as a basis for the Early Development Program of The Evan Thomas Institute which was founded under her direction upon her return to the United States in 1975.

In 1980 Janet Doman became the Vice Director of The Institutes and in 1982 she became the Director.

Her reputation as an authority on both well and brain-injured children is internationally recognized and she is a much-requested lecturer in Japan and in many other countries.

Janet Doman has co-authored several books in *The Gentle Revolution Series.* For her work with children she has received the "Statuette with Pedestal" awarded by the International Forum, the Brazilian Gold Medal of Honor, the Japanese *Sakura koro sho* Medal, and the British Star of Hope.

SUSAN AISEN is the Director of The Institute for the Achievement of Intellectual Excellence of The Institutes for the Achievement of Human Potential. She has served the children of the world in seven foreign countries and in the United States.

As Director of The Institute for the Achievement of Intellectual Excellence, Susan Aisen is responsible for both The Evan Thomas Institute, (of which she was the second director, having succeeded Janet Doman in that post) and the Institute which is responsible for creating high levels of intelligence in the hundreds of brain-injured children seen by The Institutes.

She is an international lecturer on the subject of intelligence in children on which she is an authority.

Awards for her work with children include the Gold Medal of Honor (Brazil), the Star of Hope (England), and the *Sakura koro sho* Medal (Japan).